YoungWrit

POETRY COMP

GREAT MINDS

Your World...Your Future...YOUR WORDS

From Kent Vol II
Edited by Steve Twelvetree

Young Writers

First published in Great Britain in 2005 by:
Young Writers
Remus House
Coltsfoot Drive
Peterborough
PE2 9JX
Telephone: 01733 890066
Website: www.youngwriters.co.uk

All Rights Reserved

© *Copyright Contributors 2005*

SB ISBN 1 84460 879 4

Foreword

This year, the Young Writers' 'Great Minds' competition proudly presents a showcase of the best poetic talent selected from over 40,000 up-and-coming writers nationwide.

Young Writers was established in 1991 to promote the reading and writing of poetry within schools and to the youth of today. Our books nurture and inspire confidence in the ability of young writers and provide a snapshot of poems written in schools and at home by budding poets of the future.

The thought, effort, imagination and hard work put into each poem impressed us all and the task of selecting poems was a difficult but nevertheless enjoyable experience.

We hope you are as pleased as we are with the final selection and that you and your family continue to be entertained with *Great Minds From Kent Vol II* for many years to come.

Contents

Beechwood Sacred Heart School
Francesca Copleston (13)   1
Lydia Harris (13)   2
Alexandra Whitehouse (11)   3
Fafa Segbefia (11)   3
Bertha Opoku-Acheampong (14)   4
Sarah Thomas (14)   4
Vanessa Cooper (14)   5
Stephanie Johnson (12)   5
Isabella Copleston (11)   6

Borden Grammar School
Christopher David Jordan (14)   6
Steven Wheeler (13)   7
Callum Wildish (13)   8
Aaron Grover (13)   8
Jonathan Webb (13)   9
Andrew Stalley (13)   10
Johnathan Rudland (14)   10
Jamie Smith (13)   11
Tim Jenkins (13)   11
Daniel Skinner (13)   12
Harry Little (13)   12
David Manning (13)   13
Aston James Wilson (14)   13
Rory Hopcraft (13)   14
Luke Grubb (13)   15
Nick Samuel (13)   16
Jacob Jeffery (13)   16
Declan Jewell (13)   17
Jake Clark (13)   17
Nicholas Dye (15)   18
Sean Melia (14)   18
Josh Browne (13)   19
Jack Parker (13)   19
Terry Brookman (13)   20
Luke Williams (14)   21
Paul Hood (14)   22
Joe Tucker (13)   23

Harvey Melia (14) 24

Broomhill Bank School
Sarah Thorn (14) 24
Katie Bull (15) 25
Ruth Archer (14) 25

Cleeve Park School
Nicola Bailes (12) 26
Tom Kerby (13) 26
John Baxter (13) 26
Danni Powell 27
Laura Beeson (12) 28

Homewood School & Sixth Form Centre
Annie Hollamby (11) 28
Lauren Walker (11) 29
Harry Shearing (12) 30
Alice Trice (12) 31
Amber Mannering (11) 32
Laura Baker (11) 32
Alexander Bowers (11) 33
Lewis Pentecost (11) 33
Martha Sears (11) 34
Sam Towers (12) 34
Hana Zureiqi (11) 35
Alice Millen (12) 35
Samantha Kinsella (12) 36
Laura Harford (12) 36
Rachel Taylor (12) 37
Soumbal Qureshi (13) 37
Ian Fleming (12) 38
Jonathan Williams (12) 39
Hannah Jolly (12) 40
Samantha Shearn (12) 40
James Fuller (12) 41
Paige Smith (12) 41
Kasia Nwansi (12) 42
Hannah Collis (12) 42
Callum Draper (13) 43
Matthew Berry (11) 44

Sophia Kearns (12)	44
Sam Da Costa (12)	45
Natasha Luckhurst (12)	45
Luke Excell (12)	46
Alfred Browning (12)	46
Lewis Thorowgood (11)	47
Louise Bugden (11)	47
Calum Farmer (12)	48
Emily Jenkins (12)	48
Kristina Norman (12)	49
Hayley McCleave (11)	49
Lucy Paige (13)	50
Luke Lawrence (11)	50
Peter Morris (13)	51
Matt Bridgeman (13)	51
Charlotte Houps (12)	52
Sophie Oliver (13)	52
Jack Mounstephen (11)	53
Louise King (12)	53
Dominic Roome (11)	54
Michelle Rogers (12)	54
Kirstin Warnett (11)	55
Harry Kelleher (12)	55
Charlie Bedwell (12)	56
Emma Wakefield (12)	57
Scarlet Wilson (11)	58
Sean Weekes (12)	58
Jake Wilson (11)	59
Thomas Reeves (12)	59
Lee Rathbone (12)	60
Adèle Purvis (13)	60
Lauren Waring (13)	61
Alysa Virani (12)	61
Robert Kirby (13)	62
Jade Pemberton (12)	62
Sophie Kimber (11)	63
Matthew Savage (12)	63
Jack Ward (11)	64
Charlie McKenzie (13)	64
Travis Paige (11)	65
Stephen Douse (11)	65
Glen Pryor (11)	66

Ryan Cooper (11)   67
Freddie Gibbs (11)   68
Charlotte Morris (11)   68
Hannah Pau (11)   69
Simone Wilson (11)   69
David Housman (11)   70
Elspeth Brown (11)   70
Kim Smith (12)   71
Chantelle Wood (12)   71
Emma Giles (11)   72
Kayleigh Hesmer (12)   72
Harry Sedden (11)   73
Jonathan Penney (12)   73
Eddie Warne (11)   74
Robert Tompsett (11)   74
Katie Dean (11)   75
James Richards (11)   75
Emma Wink (12)   76
Ashleigh Britten (11)   76
Alisha Styles (11)   77
Emily Hodgson (11)   78
Emma Rye (11)   78
David Dyer (11)   79

The Sittingbourne Community College
Stacey Roe (11)   79
Penny Seymour (12)   80
Matthew Houghten (11)   80
Kim McDermott (11)   81
Amy Freeman (11)   81
Jessica Eldridge (11)   82
Amy Webb (11)   82
Matthew Hendry (12)   83
Charlie Rochester (11)   83
Leon Gorman (13)   84
Alexandra Brookman (11)   85
Jordan Houghton (11)   85
Zoe Tyler (13)   86
Guy Cornelius (11)   86
Hollie Parkinson   87
Nathan Bibbings (13)   87

Jodie Shepherd (13)	88
Emma Warren (13)	89
Sophie Deacon (12)	90
Jodie Roberts (12)	91

The Thomas Aveling School

Mitchel Platt (13)	91
David Colbourne (11)	92
Taylor Grindley (12)	92
Sophie Baldock (12)	93
Soren Sutton (12)	93
Jennifer Taylor & Joanne Peterson (12)	94
Hannah Wallington (11)	94
Aaron de Bruin (11)	95
Matthew Jeffreys (11)	95
Tom Morgan (12)	96
Lorna Fazakerley (11)	96
Kirstin Bicker (11)	97
Lauren McLeod (11)	97
Sabrina Powar (14)	98
Johnathan Sutton (11)	98
Amy Dettmar (12)	99
Priyanka Mistry (12)	99
Katie Harden (12)	100
Alexander Rossiter (11)	100
Andreas Eliades (14)	100
John Williams (11)	101
Lizzie Cook (13)	101
Amandeep Thind (14)	101
Kuldeep Bahia (11)	102
Rosa Housby (12)	102
Sam Chapman (14)	103
Daniel Reeves (14) & Rosie Parris (13)	103
Toni Carter (13)	104
Robert O'Leary & Craig Evans (12)	104
Sam Jorba (13)	105
Tom Wadhams (15)	105
Amy English (13)	105
Kane Hallett (15)	106
Sophie Bell (14)	106
Steven Sanders (15)	106

Joe Swanborough (14)	107
Robert Gosling (14)	107
Matthew Baldock (11)	107
Danny Keane (13)	108
Jade Minchin (13)	108
Leanne Doust (13)	109
Louie Shaw (13)	109
Natasha Prendergast (13)	110
Sam Van Der Tak (12)	110
Lewis Church (12)	110
Steven Edney (12)	111
Steven Stewart (12)	111
Charlotte Hayes (11)	111
Lottie Elvin (13)	112
Joanne Cooke (14)	112
Chris O'Brien (13)	113
Kim Dhami (13)	113
Ryan Brimsted (13)	114
Alastair Hutton (13)	114
Frances Pyke (13)	114
Emma Humphrey (13)	115
Kemsley Perry (12)	115
Sonny Whiting (16)	115
Priya Vadher (13)	116
Ruth Humphrey (13)	116
Liam Bartlett (11)	117
Conor Mahoney (12)	117
Shantel Jarrett (11)	118
Arzumand Faheza Ali (12)	118
Katie Jago (12)	119
Jodie Fraser (12)	119
Levi Verrall (12)	120
Mecheala Leigh Mills (12)	120
Paige Bicker (12)	121
Abbie Holmes (12)	121
Nicole Teo (11)	122
Vickie Busher (12)	122
Alfie Mason (11)	123
Grace Barker (11)	123
Katie Dodsworth (12)	124
Emma North (13)	124
Sam Price (11)	125

Raheemul Mumin (13)	125
Kyle Rogers (11)	126
Bradley Shuter (11)	126
Kelsey Fordham (13)	127
Jennifer Cordingley (12)	127
John Luke Fright (11)	128
Chloe Bailey (13)	128
Simon Hird (13)	129
Casey Perry (14)	129
Ayulie Dabor (11)	129
Hayley Parkin (13)	130

The Poems

Autumn Wood

Where the Earth is damp and the air is cool,
Where the elfish elders are hidden in pools,
Where the dwarves and pixies play on the rocks,
And the riverside fairies weave their taffeta frocks.

Where the undergrowth spirits prepare for their ball,
And the tall tree guardians let their red leaves fall,
Where the autumn showers cause a swirling mist,
And the sound underfoot is cold and crisp.

The swamps and the clearings have a mysterious air,
And the old, moody demons guard their lairs,
Whilst the subdued birds circle overhead,
All thinking about food, all eager to be fed.

Where the conkers' spiky shells are crunched away,
By the heavy-footed trolls who stomp and sway,
While the pine cones fall from their evergreen trees,
And the thorny bushes bare the last of the blackberries.

Mistletoe replaces the apple tree's fruit,
And the harsh wind batters from branches to roots,
While the ivy creeps up the twisted oaks,
The toadstools shelter tiny wood folk.

Where the days are covered in a heavy grey cloud,
And the little robin redbreasts sit small but proud,
Whilst the holly's berries turn a deep Christmas red,
And the animals hibernate in their warm, leafy beds.

Francesca Copleston (13)
Beechwood Sacred Heart School

A Birthday In A Nursing Home

Name: Old Agnes
Age: 99¾

My skin tells my story,
Old, wrinkled and pale,
My legs made for walking,
Now tired and frail.

Another year, another wrinkle,
Is what I used to say,
To my dear old grandma,
Who's now sadly passed away.

Now years have come
And I have taken her place,
The 'Old Bat' they would say,
Some, even to my face!

Sitting in my chair,
Facing the outside lane,
To walk to that lane,
Causes agonising pain.

Because tomorrow I'm one hundred,
That day brings me glee,
My care workers may at least,
Bring me decent cup of tea!

A birthday in a nursing home,
What more could you want?
They call me 'Old Agnes'
That's all that I am.

Lydia Harris (13)
Beechwood Sacred Heart School

My Family

My family is small,
But each person valued as much as the other,
My sister is the youngest
My dad is the oldest.

We all have brown eyes and brown hair
When we go on holiday
Our hair goes a light brown
When we come home it turns dark brown again.

Our house has four bedrooms
Three bathrooms and two studies
Our house is in Heathfield
A quiet town with roadworks!

So basically we all are
One big, happy family, just having lots of fun!

Alexandra Whitehouse (11)
Beechwood Sacred Heart School

The Carnival

The sound of a carnival starts off loud and ends loud,
There's no peace and quiet,
There's people blowing whistles, people shouting,
There's loud music,
You can smell food, you see coloured lights flashing everywhere,
Children screaming, crying and making loud noises.
You may see somebody that you know taking part,
You shout their name, they see you,
They put one finger behind their ear and say
'I can't hear you,' and you're there thinking they are miming.
A carnival is loud, a carnival is fun and a
Carnival is a time for everyone.

Fafa Segbefia (11)
Beechwood Sacred Heart School

Sometimes

Sometimes you sit down and wonder, *what did I just do?*
Did I do the right thing by saying what I said?
Sometimes you wish you were rich and married to a prince,
You would have a tiara with your name on it and
People would compare you to your favourite stars.
Sometimes you think, *I could be living on the street.*
Not being able to know when your next meal was going to be,
Sometimes you see yourself getting a job as a singer,
Actor, model or a footballer but you end up working in Tesco.
Sometimes the reason is you dropped out of school
Early to give your career a head start.
Sometimes you feel stupid
Because your mother said this would happen.
What you should say to yourself is,
Life is too short, live it to the fullest.

Bertha Opoku-Acheampong (14)
Beechwood Sacred Heart School

Fear

Fear is something you create inside yourself so strong
It builds up scaring yourself even more and more
Never stay home alone
For your heart will pound
As your fear might be hanging around
The hair will prickle upon your neck and a sweat will break out
Don't panic, just jump under your bed!

Sarah Thomas (14)
Beechwood Sacred Heart School

Christmas

It's a time of joy, fun, love and happiness.
It only comes once a year and it's the best time as well.
Children playing in the snow, snowflakes gently landing
On the tree glistening in the sunlight.

Everyone is wrapped up warm by the fireplace,
Drinking egg-nog and home-made biscuits.
People visiting people's homes,
Spreading the Christmas cheer to them.
Stockings are being filled by Father Christmas.

The Christmas tree is covered in lights and balls
And holly is put in and around the house to celebrate this time of year.
It glows and shines on the eve of the year we await
And Santa brings all the gifts we have asked for
And to spend the special day with our family and loved ones.

Vanessa Cooper (14)
Beechwood Sacred Heart School

Alone

Alone in a shadowy corner, crouched in fright so alone,
A clear droplet hits the floor with a soft thud,
Your tears are your only friends,
Your inner self closes in around you,
The darkness, your blanket to keep you warm from your despair,
Your dignity fades like the light outside, which was your only hope,
In your own mind you realise that there is no end to your loneliness.

Stephanie Johnson (12)
Beechwood Sacred Heart School

A Guilty Conscience

He watches from the treetops,
He stares, upon the hill,
He dogs your every footstep,
Always there, against your will.

He whispers from your bedpost,
He's there when you awake,
He fills your head with a poisonous guilt,
Your every comfort is at stake.

His eyes, they burn into your back,
As he snakes along behind,
Twisting all your thoughts around,
Playing with your mind.

Then, as if an angel's come,
Your heavy weight is shed,
Your demon gone, your conscience cleared,
Once the apology is said.

Isabella Copleston (11)
Beechwood Sacred Heart School

Great Minds

My mind is good and bad,
My mind is happy and sad,
My mind is feeling fine,
My mind is divine,
Sometimes my mind is happy and giving,
Using my mind, I will make a living,
This is my mind and I feel great,
This is my mind and there is no hate,
My mind works during the day,
At night my mind goes grey,
My mind is perfectly fine,
My mind is always mine.

Christopher David Jordan (14)
Borden Grammar School

The Greatness Of The Mind

The way people use their minds:
Some people use their minds to do great things
But some people try to use it to its potential
You can try to be scientific or a maths professor
But if you cannot do these sort of things
It does not mean you are stupid.

Isaac Newton, he discovered gravity
And came up with a formulae to prove it
This proved how fast things should fall
He had a mind of greatness
And used his mind to its potential
He discovered and proved things until he died.

But minds are not just for science
They can be artistic
Able to design structures
You can write poems and stories
Just like I did this, it is still using my mind
This might be your mind's greatness.

Leonardo De Vinci, he used his mind to create art
He made statues and paintings
That are fascinating pieces of art
He painted the Mona Lisa
Which is a work of art
He used his mind to its potential.

Spike Milligan, he wrote poems and stories
Which were for children and adults
He got his ideas from his kids and childhood
He wrote 'On The Ning Nang Nong' and other poems
These poems were funny and excellent
He used his mind to entertain.

Steven Wheeler (13)
Borden Grammar School

Great Minds

All the great minds, all the great minds,
Sometimes hurtful, sometimes kind,
When you're hurtful, you go to war,
Always worried about the score.

You have imagined the best arts,
You invented maths, you must be smart,
You've done the big things like gone to space,
Even the little things like to tie a shoelace.

When in space, we went to the moon,
One day we will live there soon,
You invented the toilet, how hygienically cool,
Also adjectives like miniature and small.

Callum Wildish (13)
Borden Grammar School

What Brains Are?

Minds are great,
Minds are cool,
They will get you,
In a good school.

Minds make you brainy,
Minds make you smart,
Minds help you work,
So you get a good mark.

If you don't have a mind,
You're not a bright spark,
You will get rubbish grades,
Unless you push your brain hard!

Aaron Grover (13)
Borden Grammar School

Great Minds

There are great minds thinking great things sometimes,
Imagining and thinking, for example: maths, science
and even singing.

A source of power, sometimes turning good minds sour,
Minds of good, minds of bad,
Turning faces happy, turning them sad.

Minds of depth, knowledge and power,
People have only scraped the surface,
If only we could discover them more - pure bliss!

Dreams, things our mind is trying to say, nobody
understands dreams, OK?
Perplex, in a time zone of its own,
From when you dream in your sleep, in your bed at home,
Mostly flashes and long stories that seem to go on for ages.

Controlling emotions and things like that:
Making us happy, making us want to wear hats,
Also making us . . . erm . . . love cats?

I am going to leave you thinking,
Thinking about what I have written,
Or thinking that your mind is thinking that you are
thinking about thinking,
Anyway I am running out of words to rhyme,
So I'll say goodbye, until next time.

So in conclusion, I know they are complex,
I'm going now, I wonder whose poem is next?

Jonathan Webb (13)
Borden Grammar School

The Human Mind

The human mind is a fireworks display,
Always changing, loud and bright,
The mind is a computer,
Always processing data,
The mind hardly stops,
Always finding things to do,
The mind is dangerous,
Thinking up dangerous things,
The mind is wonderful,
Keeping us alive,
The mind is inventive,
Always coming up with new ideas,
The mind is a tool,
Always used,
The mind is thirsty,
For old and new,
The mind is all these things,
And more,
The mind can do great good,
Or great evil.

Andrew Stalley (13)
Borden Grammar School

Great Minds!

Great minds think alike,
Shame I don't think like anyone else,
De Vinci, Galileo, Dickens, Edison,
Helicopter, telescope, Great Expectations, the light bulb,
All came from their mind,
If I could have a great mind like this,
I would get an A in DT,
In future I will have a great mind,
From school, the world and experience,
I will have a great mind.

Johnathan Rudland (14)
Borden Grammar School

The Shoot-out

The sky was full of clouds,
As the fog was drawing in,
The shoot-out was about to start,
The cowboys drew their guns,
They were 30 metres apart,
The fog was filling the surrounding air,
And vision was so much harder,
The shoot-out began,
The noise was terrifying,
Bang, bang went the guns,
Then a crowd started to appear,
Cheering occurred by crowd members,
Shopkeepers came out of their shops,
Barmen walked out the saloon,
The village blacksmith appeared out from his workshop,
All to see the action
Bang, bang once again,
The firing was non-stop,
The crowd was showing all emotions,
Then the shoot out stopped
A sudden silence . . .

Jamie Smith (13)
Borden Grammar School

Where's Your Brain Boy?

'Boy in the corner.'
There was a sudden jerk,
'Yes Sir, sorry Sir.'
'The board boy.'
'5Y+3Z Sir,' he said.
'Wrong boy,
Where's your brain today?'
'Sorry Sir.'
'Did you leave it in bed?
Think boy think.'

Tim Jenkins (13)
Borden Grammar School

Fishy Thoughts

The mind is a wonderful fish,
He swims around in your head,
Looking for a knowledge dish,
Oh how he loves to be fed,
He wants to show everyone,
How smart he really is,
This is how he has some fun,
All of your thoughts are his.
The mind is a wonderful fish,
He swims around in your head,
Looking for a knowledge dish,
Oh how he loves to be fed,
He could make up stories,
From far across the sea,
He doesn't like Tories,
And he's in you and me,
Oh yes, the mind is a wonderful fish.

Daniel Skinner (13)
Borden Grammar School

The Mind Of A Genius

The mind of a genius, what must that be like?
An everlasting journey or arduous hike?
Like a thousand light bulbs switching on and off,
But it comes with the price of being called a boff.

The mind of a genius always knows the right answer,
Like the precision used by a professional dancer,
Thoughts and ideas arrive throughout the day and night,
Turned into knowledge with amazing foresight.

The mind of a genius, it constantly evolves,
Continually finding new problems to solve,
Like a battery's life can become corroded,
A genius mind can become overloaded.

Harry Little (13)
Borden Grammar School

Great Minds

G reat minds come in many different forms,
R eading can help to create great mind,
E dward Elgar had a great industrial mind,
A lbert Einstein also had a great mind because
        he was the man who discovered gravity.
T here is an old saying, which is, 'Great minds think alike.'

M ickey Mouse is the creation of a great mind,
I f you went to school, you could also have a great mind,
N ormally great minds come with hard work,
D arwin devoted his lifetime to understanding the theory
        of natural selection.
S o now you know that great minds come in many different
forms such as being good at maths, science or devoting a
lifetime to something important.

David Manning (13)
Borden Grammar School

Great Minds

Einstein discovered $E = MC^2$,
Newton understood weight,
Shakespeare wrote fantastic plays,
Leonardo planned flying machines,
Edison made the light bulb,
Galileo invented the telescope,
Columbus found America,
Belle made the telephone,
Hawkings discovered the black hole,
Aristotle did philosophy,
Groening thought of the The Simpsons,
But each journey started with a single step.

Aston James Wilson (14)
Borden Grammar School

Great Minds

Leonardo Da Vinci had a great mind,
Painting the Mona Lisa's smile,
Designing a flying machine that no one knew.

Charles Darwin had a great mind,
Species of animals and plants too,
His very book read by millions of you.

William Shakespeare had a great mind,
Writing romance everyone loves,
Plays played at The Globe loved and lived by you.

Sir Isaac Newton had a great mind,
The lump on the head by a fateful apple,
The laws of gravity never defined.

Alexandra Graham Bell had a great mind,
The long way telephone call you use now,
Over sea, over land, as far, as wide that's the new distance.

Winston Churchill had a great mind,
Planning the war with his great mind,
Winnie the Pooh with a cigarette in hand.

Adolf Hitler had a great mind,
Dictating with power and mind with ease
World War II, all his doing in failure.

David Bailey had a great mind,
Photos here, photos there, photos on his calm, cool mind,
His world of shocking truth by a photographical image.

Charles Dickens had a great mind,
Thinking hard and thinking straight, pen to paper,
Creating masterpieces we all enjoy reading.

I have a great mind,
Thinking of those difficult questions,
What? Where? When? You think hard, you decide.

Rory Hopcraft (13)
Borden Grammar School

A Great Mind

The mind is hungry,
Hungry for information,
Information to be collected,
Collected in mass.

The mind is searching,
Searching for answers,
Answers to questions,
Questions untold.

The mind is power,
Power for leadership,
Leadership to continue,
Continue in life.

The mind is unique,
Unique in its existence,
Existence for knowledge,
Knowledge more facts.

The mind is imaginative,
Imaginative in colour,
Colour to picture,
Picture the memories.

The mind is destructive,
Destructive in warfare,
Warfare for freedom,
Freedom to exist.

The mind is inspirational,
Inspirational as creative,
Creative is challenging,
Challenging great minds.

Luke Grubb (13)
Borden Grammar School

Great Minds

I would like to be an inventor,
And invent something new,
I would like to be an inventor,
And forever stop flu.

I would like to be an inventor,
And make inventing cool,
I would like to be an inventor,
And get to miss school.

I would like to be clever,
And get a decent job,
I would like to be clever,
And help my mate, Bob.

I would like to be clever,
And get good marks,
I would like to be clever,
But I don't know where to start!

Nick Samuel (13)
Borden Grammar School

Great Minds

There was a man who was kind,
He had a very good mind,
He was very clever,
He's as light as a feather,
His name is Sebastian Heinze.

Sebastian Heinze,
His IQ is very high,
He is . . . amazing.

M ike is Sebastian's best friend,
I think they'll be friends till the end,
N othing is out of his reach,
D oes anything confuse him?
S am says 'Definitely not!'

Jacob Jeffery (13)
Borden Grammar School

Great Minds

G rammar minds are always very useful,
R emarkable minds are too,
E ars, not mouths, should be used at school,
A lthough it is sometimes hard,
T o keep your mouth shut.

P oems come in different categories,
O r really they should,
E very poem doesn't have to rhyme,
T hough it can be more humorous,
R eally good vocabulary should be used in poems,
Y es, poetry is very exciting.

M any poems do rhyme,
I do enjoy writing poetry,
N ormally poems take only a few lines,
D on't you like poems?
S uppose you won't know because you haven't tried!

Declan Jewell (13)
Borden Grammar School

Three Great Minds

Kelly Holmes was the one to make Britain proud,
Both times she won, wild went the crowd,
She won two medals of gold, it was a sight to behold,
The celebrations were long and loud.

There was a rapper called Jay-Z,
His music was the best, his lyrics crazy,
One of the best rappers there was, now he's quit that job,
Now he's going out with Beyoncé, lucky sod.

Wayne Rooney was the saviour of Euro 2004,
Every game we saw, he would frequently score,
He is Britain's brightest new star, definitely and by far,
He's got the public wanting more.

Jake Clark (13)
Borden Grammar School

Great Minds

They say that great minds
Think alike,
Then someone tell me why?
The greatest scientists can't agree,
However hard they try!

'The Earth is flat,'
No, no it's round!'
'Do we move through the sky?'
'Of course we don't!
We stand quite still,
It's the sun that's passing by.'

The statement then is groundless,
No, wait perhaps it's true,
As, if all the great minds can't agree
Then they're all agreeing too!

Nicholas Dye (15)
Borden Grammar School

Great Minds

Everyone has a brain,
Some are good, some are bad,
But they all have one thing in common,
They all think.

Some famous people depend on their minds,
Some don't,
But most of them are used to do great things,
Like create electricity and the telephone.

Everyone needs a brain to live,
To think and to have control,
Everyone is unique,
Because they think in their own separate ways.

Sean Melia (14)
Borden Grammar School

Poetry Day

G reat poetry all day long,
R eally interesting and amusing,
E very day it goes your way,
A lways reminding you poetry is there,
T houghtful and colourful in their own way.

P oems are fun and exciting,
O ver and over again,
E very day it fills your mind,
T here are poems around.
R eally happy and full of life,
Y es poems are always around.

M iraculous, filling the mind,
I nteresting and cool, these are poems,
N ever disappointing, always approved,
D oing what they should, making a rhyme.
S uper and sunny poems around.

Josh Browne (13)
Borden Grammar School

Great Minds

The flame of the great mind burns
Continually day and night
Their own ability
A custodian to themselves
But the stress and anger
Is what will extinguish the flame
For madness and their own superiority
Will creep in
Their own success
A punishment
Their standards to themselves
Stretch their sanity
Distorting life
For only them
They are alone.

Jack Parker (13)
Borden Grammar School

Imagination To Think Ahead

I start with a little thing
The beginning
Imagine this, a mind
Ours is clever, leaves others behind,
But it's because we can think ahead,
That's the reason we sleep in a bed.

It is because we have imagination,
That's the key to every invention,
A person can have a mind, no other greater,
But imagination makes an inventor.

That's the reason our species survived,
Whereas Neanderthal man, they all died,
An imagination is the key to survival,
A truly great mind has one, no denial.

Look at all the famous minds,
Newton, Archimedes and Einstein,
Imagination, to think ahead was the key,
To each personal victory.

So it is this imagination,
That led to our survival,
So do our ancestors a favour and
Give ice cream a new flavour.

Terry Brookman (13)
Borden Grammar School

You Don't Know What's Going Through Their Heads

The whistle went, it had come, my turn.
I walked towards it, I walked as slow as I could.
I felt a pain or fright going through me.
This was it, the decider of the match.

I stood there looking at the ball,
Then I looked up, there he was, the enemy.
He looked as frightened as I felt,
I was so scared I could hardly breathe.

The ref looked at me, I looked back,
I was now as scared as ever.
He looked at the keeper, he nodded,
He raised his hand towards his mouth,
I knew this was it.

As the whistle went, I looked at the ball,
Then at the keeper, he was ready and waiting,
I took my first step, then the next,
This was it, I hit it as hard as I could.

I opened my eyes,
It was sitting in the back of the net.
I could hear the crowd again,
I had done it, we had won.

Luke Williams (14)
Borden Grammar School

The Great Minds

With Einstein to Newton who invented things we use
They found out about lightning and other things too,
One of those is gravity which everybody has to use,
But if these people didn't find out about these things
Then we would not know now.

Everybody uses inventions as there are new things every single day,
But some people take these inventions for granted,
Which is destroying where we live,
We have cars and bikes, both an invention in themselves
But they both use an invention of its own and that has
Revolutionised the world.

We have the wheel that was invented by the Romans
It has revolutionised the world.
We use it for most transportation and have made it out
Of all sorts of things,
We use it to race and we use it to carry but these things are
Essential for our everyday life.

As we use the wheels for everything from cars to trains
To trolleys, if we didn't have the wheel then we would never
Have been able to change -
For farming we would still be using the cattle and cart
And never would have changed the way we live and cut our crops.

Paul Hood (14)
Borden Grammar School

Minds . . . Minds . . . Minds

Minds . . . minds . . . minds . . .
Clever brains, clever minds,
Complicated, confusing, wonderful,
How do they work?
What happens to them?
Nobody knows!
It's so confusing,
Think about it,
Or brain is trying to work out how all brains in general work,
Confused?
Where do we start?
Great thinkers are baffled by how we work,
Yet know more about objects in space millions of miles away,
Take Stephen Hawkings,
The most intelligent man on Earth,
Has PHDs in science,
But doesn't know everything known to man,
Many people know things no one else on Earth does,
Minds must work together to gather all this knowledge,
Knowledge of everything known to man.

Joe Tucker (13)
Borden Grammar School

This Person

This person has a mind of knowledge,
Their head full of amazing facts,
This person has a mind of value,
Making sure it's kept intact.

This person has a mind of answers,
And questions that they'll ask as well,
This person has a mind of grammar,
Able to write and also spell.

This person has a mind of memories,
From the distant past and present too,
This person has a mind of greatness,
This person . . . is you!

Harvey Melia (14)
Borden Grammar School

The Cat

Grey all over, purrs,
Sits on my lap,
Feels lovely, short soft fur,
Mouse catcher,
Time to feed him
'Miaow,'
'Get that mouse out!'
Cries Mum.

Sarah Thorn (14)
Broomhill Bank School

The Mysterious Path

Standing in the orchard
Cherry trees glowing, swaying wind
Rushing with the leaves
I find the magic path
I walk and walk
Evergreen with the wet dew
I stand and stare.
Picking juicy fruits
I feel the glorious sun setting on my face.
The path is fading
Trees are going, sun is sinking
Evergreens are still there
But trees seem bare, wind is howling, scary
I wish the path would show
I want the path to guide me home,
In the middle of this dark green orchard
Feel air in my hair, dew on my feet
Sadness,
I hope the path will come back soon
Tired of this wood
Wishing I could find my way home.

Katie Bull (15)
Broomhill Bank School

A Prayer For Children

Children please be calm,
Children please don't cry,
Children please close your eyes,
Do not worry.

Children I will be there,
Children I will look after you,
Children I will love you,
Forever and ever.

Ruth Archer (14)
Broomhill Bank School

I Dream

I dreamt I was an angel,
Flying swiftly through the air
I'd bring peace throughout the land
And the lions' lair.

I dreamt I was a pilot,
Flying higher than the sun
Going round and round and round
Oh what fun.

I dreamt I was an athlete,
Running, running, running,
Winning all the medals,
How cunning.

I dreamt I was a lion,
No, a baby girl,
But the best thing is, I am me!

Nicola Bailes (12)
Cleeve Park School

The Otter

The otter gracefully swam through the misty waters,
The stars shone brightly,
The moon was a bedrock of diamonds,
The sun was greatness bleached with lemon.

Tom Kerby (13)
Cleeve Park School

Battle Noises

Battle drums thumping,
Battle cries chanting,
Wounded moaning,
Wounded crying,
Dead lying still, silence, still.

John Baxter (13)
Cleeve Park School

A New Beginning

I woke up on Tuesday morning,
When I got a bit of a fright,
It wasn't the same as I went to bed,
On Monday night.

I left for school,
At half-past eight,
But when I got there,
I was really, really late.

We lined up in the playground,
And when I went into the school,
We gazed out of the window,
To watch the snow fall.

We went out to play,
To build a snowman,
And to throw snowballs,
Until it was banned.

I woke up on Wednesday morning,
It was very, very bright,
It wasn't the same as I went to bed,
On Tuesday night.

Danni Powell
Cleeve Park School

Got To Tidy My Room Today

Can't go out until I've tidied my room,
Can't go out until it's spotless,
It's a Saturday,
But there's no time to play,
Got to tidy my room today,
My room feels like a death trap,
Everywhere you look it's a mess,
My bed's not made,
There are clothes on the floor,
It's a Saturday,
But there's no time to play,
Got to tidy my room today.

Laura Beeson (12)
Cleeve Park School

Inside My Head

I nside my head there are lots of questions,
N obody can answer.
S tuff that is made up,
I have a lot of jokes inside my head too,
D ifferent kinds of animals and made up games,
E verything is inside my head.

M emories inside my head are one thing nobody can take,
Y esterday is another memory inside my head.

H appy memories and sad memories are inside my head,
E very day another memory is put inside my head,
A s you can see my head is full of different things,
D aydreaming is another one.

Annie Hollamby (11)
Homewood School & Sixth Form Centre

Inside My Head

Inside my head it is dark,
Nobody in there to make their mark,
Candles are its only light,
So as you can see, it's not very bright.

Inside my head there is a dream,
Even that isn't as it seems,
To be a musician, a photographer, a teacher,
I'm so confused on choosing a future.

Inside my head there are pictures of my friends,
Memories that I know are not pretend,
I hope that through all our school years,
There will not be many tears.

Inside my head there is a fear,
On whether my future will have a good career,
I hope I do, I'm just unsure,
Will there ever be a proper cure?

Inside my head there is a memory of my first bike ride,
I told Dad I knew where the brakes were, I lied.
I gave myself a great big push,
When suddenly I crashed into a thorn bush!

Inside my head there are some thoughts,
Some are long and interesting whereas some are dull and short,
One of my thoughts is if my homework is done for today,
Otherwise a detention will come my way.

Lauren Walker (11)
Homewood School & Sixth Form Centre

My Great Mind

Inside my mind there is a Lotus Elise,
And a journey
To the top of Mount Everest.

There's a sparkling ocean,
So clear it's like air,
On the east coast of Spain.

Where the sun is so bright,
It shines straight through you,
Like slivers of glass.

A trip to Las Vegas,
In the desert,
To the richest casino ever.

I hope to be a millionaire,
A swimming pool full of money,
And own the biggest yacht.

There are golden escalators,
Shiny as a mirror,
Leading forever on end.

My mind is full of adventures,
And my journey has only just begun.

Harry Shearing (12)
Homewood School & Sixth Form Centre

Great Minds

'Great minds think alike'
Or so the saying goes,
Great minds are people who
Are always in the know.
Great minds keep working
Really, really fast,
And like to know things
Especially from the past.
Great minds like to recite,
And know all about William Shakespeare's
'Midsummer's Night Dream,'
And I like to watch scary films,
The ones that make you *scream!*

Great minds find it easy to study,
Although their minds are always in a hurry,
They're interested in science, history and biology,
And go on to study at Oxford University,
Grown-ups with great minds,
Sometimes work in psychology,
Great minds seldom have a rest,
I have a great mind,
And I like putting it to the test.

Alice Trice (12)
Homewood School & Sixth Form Centre

A Girl's Head

In my head is family
And a big mansion
For when I hope to become famous.

And there is
A fast sports car,
When I become rich.

And there is
A person singing,
A person acting,
A person dancing.

There is a studio,
That is metallic inside.

And it just can't be better.

I believe,
Nothing could be better than what I already have.

I hope that when I'm older, I become famous,
And have a big mansion and a fast sports car.

Amber Mannering (11)
Homewood School & Sixth Form Centre

An Imagination

Inside an imagination, there are amazing thoughts of . . .

Love and romance, sadness and laughter, the wonders of feelings,
A new creation from God's hands like a bird so small
But so many colours of the Earth.
Nature like rivers flowing in a million directions and
Trees of blue and a sky of green,
There is music, pop, classic, tunes, tweets and whistles,
A lovely sound.
There are wise and thoughtful effects like a poem of so much
Imagination, so much creation and lastly a brain.

Laura Baker (11)
Homewood School & Sixth Form Centre

Great Minds

Sometimes I think, *what's my future?*
What's my fate?
But most of the time I think of my hopes,
My dreams, like the dream to fly.
Soaring with the birds, floating in the sky,
With the wind in my face, but that's just a dream.

Adventure is my game
From the tips of Mount Everest
Or walking from one side of the world to the other
But that's just a dream.

Fear is at the tip of my mind,
Destruction, theft and death,
The most frightening things are that.

Alexander Bowers (11)
Homewood School & Sixth Form Centre

A Dog's Mind

I wonder when I am going for a walk,
All she does is talk, talk, talk,
As I gaze up to the stars,
My eyes spot the chocolate bars.

As I bark to go out,
I see a cat walking about,
What I want to do is chase that moggy,
Shall I go out? It's very foggy.

I'll just curl up in my bed,
I have had some water and been fed,
Finally, she's off the phone,
I think I'll go and find my bone.

Lewis Pentecost (11)
Homewood School & Sixth Form Centre

My Head

Inside my head there is
A whole new world where
Ghosts are holographic projections
And I am a world famous fashion designer
With my own label!

I want to live in a large house with a pool,
I want to be able to hug the big teddy bear of
The 5th floor in Harrods, every day.

I have leant loads more things,
Than I have done before,
I came to my new school,
Inside my head the old world is dead.

I am sitting in a classroom with words
And numbers spinning in my head,
I know I will change the subject but I have to jump up,
High, to reach the clouds above me,
Till eventually I drop back down, to reach the
Ground until another night.

Martha Sears (11)
Homewood School & Sixth Form Centre

What Would The World Be Like Without Water?

What would the world be like without water?
Maybe like the Ripper inflicting his slaughter,
It would be like a thorn of a rose,
And like a hole getting bigger and will never close,
There would be no cure to fire,
And water would become everyone's desire,
So give us our water, give us what we need,
So life can go on, and life can proceed.

Sam Towers (12)
Homewood School & Sixth Form Centre

A Thought In My Mind On A Dark Night!

Going up a deep, dark hill makes
Me feel like I'm on top of a dolphin,
As we go down we gradually dive deeply into
The ocean, sea.

Street lights flicker as they look like
Sunflowers drooping down, dropping dead,
Shining with brightness.

People walking as it gets darker and darker,
They form a deep black shadow like
A ghost tiptoeing behind you.

Trees swaying side to side, looking
Like a monster crowding
Its big fierce claws are over you
Whilst getting the creeps.

Scary thoughts cross my mind
As it spreads and awaits the next mystery
Person still yet to come.

Hana Zureiqi (11)
Homewood School & Sixth Form Centre

Great Minds

G reat minds think of great thoughts
R oam through rivers of ideas
E mpty spaces filling up
A mazing dreams my mind thinks up
T roublesome mind thinking troublesome thoughts.

M emories from the past coming back to haunt you.
I nside that head, what does it look like, what does it do?
N ever-ending maze stuffed inside your head
D ecisions, decisions, why won't they stop?
S taying up all night, my mind keeps ticking, ticking.

Alice Millen (12)
Homewood School & Sixth Form Centre

My Friend And I

I have a good friend,
She likes big snails,
We went to the woods one day,
She fell into a stream,
Got soaked through,
So I took her home,
And we both had tea.

I went to school,
The very next day,
I learnt what longitude and
Latitude meant,
I felt quite pleased
For now I know,
And I won't forget.

For my future,
I hope I'm rich,
Have a good life and
Live till I'm 99.

Samantha Kinsella (12)
Homewood School & Sixth Form Centre

My Mind

My head is full of dreams and thoughts,
Like my sister getting bullied at school,
My dream is to work with animals
And to have a lovely house.
My memory is my cat Jade
She was very cuddly,
I have learnt what a pre-modifier is at school,
I think what we are going to do every day,
I think about all of my family every day,
I have met a lot of people,
Since I moved into high school,
I hope one day I will have all these
Dreams and thoughts come true.

Laura Harford (12)
Homewood School & Sixth Form Centre

Inside My Mind

F unny mind, full of weird thoughts,
U nusual thoughts like, *Why is grass green?* I've never been taught.
N ormal thoughts like, *Dancing is my ambition*,
N ever ever said.
Y ellow is my favourite colour, will it never ever change?

M y mind helps me get through life,
I nside my mind are ambitions and dreams.
N obody in my class is quiet, they're all loud.
D oes the Earth move, or do the clouds?

M y mind is full of green,
Y et things that I haven't seen.

M ulticoloured dresses, does 'Celtic' give you a clue?
I rish dancing came out of the blue
N ever said, that's what I wanna be
D oesn't matter now, my mind can be free.

Rachel Taylor (12)
Homewood School & Sixth Form Centre

My Great Mind

M ind is a great thing,
Y our mind controls your every action,

G reat for planning devious schemes,
R ed, blue, pink and green thoughts,
E verlasting thoughts,
A lways working like a machine,
T imes that you can remember

M emories are in my mind
I ntelligent mind that thinks about school,
N uisance mind that thinks about funfairs,
D oes my mind ever break down. No?

I don't think so!

Soumbal Qureshi (13)
Homewood School & Sixth Form Centre

My Mind (Which Is Great)

My mind is like a maze,
Each thought reaches me,
Like a bird migrating to its destination,
I'm not sure what my mind is,
Sometimes it makes me wonder,
Who am I and what am I?

What if? Is what I think a lot
How? Who? Where? And when?
What if I will die tomorrow?
What if the world ends?
Life may not exist,
Who knows, we may be a thought from a little child's mind.

Sometimes I get scared of movies,
And they sometimes make me think,
I'm gonna get killed tonight,
By the monster that gave me a fright,
And sometimes my mind takes me elsewhere,
In the middle of a lesson.

What if our minds were a computer,
That sits on a desk each day
And one day that computer will break down,
Bringing the end of me,
Or maybe we are a book,
Being read by a parent to their child.

Ian Fleming (12)
Homewood School & Sixth Form Centre

The Weird Mind Of Mine

My mind is something I can't get to grips with.
I think of mostly horrible things,
Like people I know dying,
The horror film I watched last night,
The goriest video game I have at home.
I also think of weird things,
Like lots of things that defy logic,
But logic only exists when people do.

When I'm older, I could be a writer,
Expressing the stories which appear in my head.

My mind can be manic,
I think of doing rebellious things,
Like running in the road screaming and shouting
Until the police come to get me.
I think of burning the school down!
Don't worry, I doubt it will happen.

Ghosts may be around us, but we never know.
If I get scared on a roller coaster,
I realise I could die anytime and just enjoy it.

But then I realise that this could just be a dream
In my head, in my mum's stomach,
Which makes me want to stay in my bed
Forever, and ever, and ever . . .

Jonathan Williams (12)
Homewood School & Sixth Form Centre

My Thinking Mind

In my thinking mind, my mind ticks back and forth.
I hope we have PE and art,
So we can have lots of fun at school today.
I play with my kitten every single day,
I pick her up in the morning
And sleep with her at night.
Peanut is the best, better than the rest.
She wakes me up and nibbles on my ear
And sleeps in my bed.
I love to dance around the house
And turn the music up all night.
I would love to fly to France
And dance on a boat.
I love my family lots and lots
Because they are caring,
So here I am telling you about my life,
And what I would like to do in my life.

Hannah Jolly (12)
Homewood School & Sixth Form Centre

Great Minds

G reat minds think of great things
R emember great things
E ngage in great things
A nd arrange great things
T wo great minds make a brilliant mind.

M inds put together come up with the best of ideas
I ndividual minds think of new things
N ever-ending, interesting thoughts
D reams that come true because they're made true
S taying great and never any less.

Samantha Shearn (12)
Homewood School & Sixth Form Centre

My Mind

My memory is like a bag of sweets,
The sour sweets are my hurt,
The sharp pain of sour, that reminds me of pain.
The sugary sweets that make you tingle
Can be my funny times,
Like laughing in my mother's arms,
Or opening presents.
Those chewy sweets that are in your mouth for ages
Are my recall of growing up, always there, sometimes rages.
Soft and tender are marshmallows,
Like my times of good fun and cuddles.
A time that I remember is going fishing with my uncle.
Each memory's a present,
A colourful sweet is a hope or a dream,
Like to become a good dad, or become a graphics designer.

James Fuller (12)
Homewood School & Sixth Form Centre

Great Minds

G reat minds think alike
R ound and round in my head, like the wheels on my bike
E very day I think similar things
A t the stroke of midnight, I feel I have wings
T wo great minds make a brilliant mind.

M emories I will always remember
I magine your future, imagine mine, it might be April or
　　　　　　　　　　　　　　　　　it might be September
N ever-ending thoughts floating in my head
D reaming away when I'm in bed
S eeing the world before my eyes!

Paige Smith (12)
Homewood School & Sixth Form Centre

Great Minds
(Just for Ella)

Cherubic smile, coquettish glance,
Grins and chuckles, toes advance.

She's bonny and blithe, good and gay.
As a Monday's child she's fair of face,
A vision of Heaven in ribbons and lace.

Our little Ella, 9 months old
She's more to us than silver and gold.
In years to come she'll break the chain,
When womanhood she does attain.

Meanwhile we'll love these baby years,
Sharing her laughter, joy and tears.

Kasia Nwansi (12)
Homewood School & Sixth Form Centre

Daydreamer

When I wake up in the morning I wish I was still dreaming.
I open the curtains and there's the sun gleaming.
Immediately my mind is blown away,
I think, *my God, what a beautiful day.*
I sometimes think I am still sleeping,
Then I think while my eyes are weeping,
Is reality really all that bad?
Or is my mind just full of sad?
Then suddenly I hear a beeping sound
And I feel my feet touch the ground.
Was I asleep or was I daydreaming?
I shall never know while I watch the sun gleaming.

Hannah Collis (12)
Homewood School & Sixth Form Centre

Great Minds

Great minds are not easy to find
Shakespeare, Darwin, all one of a kind
Never a blank or empty brain
One dull moment can drive them insane.

Then there are men like Thierry Henry
Whose amazing talent fills us with glee
The speed he runs and his quick feet
Plus the determination not to be beat.

Not just men but women too
The first female PM might give you a clue
How brave that lady must have been
Imagine the things she must have seen.

What about Picasso, the famous artist?
So calm and patient, not necessarily the fastest
He delights people with his paintings
That will never be able to achieve the same things.

The Simpsons was invented by Matt Groening
That should have stopped Homer from constantly moaning
For years he's pleased children from comics and TV
Now they've made models for both you and me.

Some quite terrific people, I'm sure you'd agree
All a credit to the world and fantastic to see
Still if you work hard and never hold back
You could be a great mind too, what's better than that?

Callum Draper (13)
Homewood School & Sixth Form Centre

What's In My Mind

In my mind
another thought has
pushed its way in.

I am thinking about
going to the park
on Saturday.

I am thinking,
I wish the next lesson
would come quicker
because I have PE.

There are more things
to think about
than Thorpe Park.

I wish death
would never come
because the world
is too good to be true.

In my mind
I wish my bike
would turn up
on my doorstep.

Matthew Berry (11)
Homewood School & Sixth Form Centre

I Believe

I believe anyone can have a great mind.
You can have a great mind if you understand,
If you let teachers and parents give you a hand.
If you can believe that, you can do anything
And enjoy the knowledge that the world can bring.
There are people who have to try really hard,
And others who are just really smart.
I believe anyone can have a great mind.

Sophia Kearns (12)
Homewood School & Sixth Form Centre

A Dream

I have a dream, when I am older
To be rich with a nice car,
Not to be a low life,
Drinking in a bar.

I want to own a mansion
On seven continents,
I want to travel to the moon,
Where only Armstrong went.

I want to have a plane
To fly me different places,
Travel down to Hollywood,
Meet many famous faces.

Everyone would know my face,
for my huge economy,
Maybe buy a massive yacht
To take me out to sea.

I want to go deep-sea diving
In the coral reef,
I want to swim with great white sharks,
Even count their teeth.

Sam Da Costa (12)
Homewood School & Sixth Form Centre

Geek

His work was always neat,
His work was always right,
His work was always on the wall,
His work was never hard.

All my friends, they teased him,
But for me, I just felt sorry,
For the boy who has a great mind
And now his work is always hard.

Natasha Luckhurst (12)
Homewood School & Sixth Form Centre

My Mind's A Roller Coaster

My mind is a roller coaster
With twists, turns and drops
Memories fly by, new ones make the track
With dark memories in a huge tunnel
And good memories soar by.
The photo flash of the camera, the picture store in my mind
People I know screaming in those cars behind.
The ride never ends
For life is a roller coaster, let's get a-riding
The break strip is far
With slow parts and fast parts and parts that make you scream,
But it never breaks down, it's a continuous ride,
Non-stop soaring, day and night,
Over loops, under ground,
Not to forget up and down,
But in all it is so great, I can't wait to see what's ahead.
So come on now, let's get inside
And take a ride on the best ride.
My mind is a roller coaster
And it never ends.

Luke Excell (12)
Homewood School & Sixth Form Centre

My Manic Mind

M y mind is a pain
Y o-yoing with ideas

M y mind is a pain
A lways buzzing like a bee
N ever resting
I wonder what it does when I sleep
C ausing me to dream

M y mind is a beautiful thing
I t generates games of fun
N ever stops growing with thoughts
D ie it will, but my mind will be free.

Alfred Browning (12)
Homewood School & Sixth Form Centre

Sporting Hero

He wakes up in the ice-cold mornings and goes to train.
He is self-disciplined and committed to his job.
Snow, ice, rain or wind,
Whatever the weather he still has to train.
He did it for the Olympics,
To take part for this country,
Because he wanted to do it so much.
In his mind he knows that he can move up a level.

We are sort of similar,
He loves riding his bike and so do I.
When I come back from school
I ride my bike out and around the estate.
He will always be better than I will,
But I still look up to him.

He is the world champion at the Keirin.
He has won medals for our country.
Every year he pushes himself to get more awards.
He is great,
He is the best,
He is Jamie Staff and he is the best.

Lewis Thorowgood (11)
Homewood School & Sixth Form Centre

Greece

Golden and sandy beaches,
Hot, warm, swimming pools,
Fresh fish from the sea.
Flowing skirts and beady tops.
Water slides all day long,
Dancing, music, iced Coca-Cola.
The blazing sunshine all day long.
Old buildings, dark and grey.

Louise Dugden (11)
Homewood School & Sixth Form Centre

My Mind!

My mind is a twisted machine,
Never stops working, day or night.
It has three switches,
One for my legs,
One for my arms,
And one for my face.
It will always work,
Day and night.
It is slimy like a slug,
Slowly thinking, slowly working.
It is also like a bomb,
Always exploding with ideas and thoughts.
It will always be ticking,
Waiting to explode with those
Horrible thoughts and ideas
Ticking away in my mind.

Calum Farmer (12)
Homewood School & Sixth Form Centre

Great Minds

G reat minds are all around but most have sadly died.
R ound the whole wide world, many are around
E instein, Newton, Darwin, Shakespeare
A nd many more, but sadly most have died
T o think that they were not so famous before they died.

M aybe they wanted to die to show the world what they were
I n the world, wherever they are, I bet they wish they were alive
N ever again will they come back, but just watch us
D eath is not a nice thing, you never know when it will happen
S o watch every step, look after your mind and make the most
of your life.

Emily Jenkins (12)
Homewood School & Sixth Form Centre

My Mind Is . . .

My mind is a bubble
Of clothes and shoes.
An explosion of pink,
What top? How can I choose?

In my room
There's rows and rows
Of colourful shoes,
With a wardrobe of clothes.

My secret diary,
All fluffy and pink.
Open the lock,
You'll have a shock.

It holds my secrets
And all of my lies.
Who I fancy,
And when I cry.

All my walls are baby pink,
With my fluffy rug.
All the teddies
That I hug.

Kristina Norman (12)
Homewood School & Sixth Form Centre

The Chameleon

Slowly walks as quiet as can be,
Confidently walks, lurching for food.
Nervously hiding in case of a fright,
Briskly camouflaging for the autumn to come,
Sharply resting for a quiet sleep,
Hissing angrily for getting impatient,
Quietly watching the water trickle,
As it carefully plunges for its attack.

Hayley McCleave (11)
Homewood School & Sixth Form Centre

My Mind

My mind is a thick piece of twisted pasta,
Turned and twisted in all sorts of places
With all kinds of knowledge
Attached to the frazzled ends.
My mind is like an explorer,
Trying to find out new things every day.
My mind is like a clock, *tick-tock,* ticking away.
My thoughts are all locked away,
Though they want to get out
And tell the world all my ideas.

My thoughts are locked in my head,
Which is exactly 21.5 inches round.
They bounce back and forth
Like a bouncy ball making lots of sound.
My mind is like a sergeant major
Telling me what to do,
Marching around inside my head,
Making my ideas stick to my brain like glue.

Lucy Paige (13)
Homewood School & Sixth Form Centre

Football Crazy

Smashing the ball, swerving through the air,
Flying like a Concorde down the right wing,
Then he furiously gets tackled.
It's a penalty.
The crowd go wild, like a million lions,
The tension of taking a penalty.
He runs, he shoots, he scores,
The relief of the final whistle,
The rush you feel flowing through your veins.

Luke Lawrence (11)
Homewood School & Sixth Form Centre

The Whispering Mutter

The night draws in, the stars so bright,
The wind it howls through the night.
Silhouettes appear and fade away.
The ghostly night is now in sight.

I sit on the bench by the cobbled street,
Candlelight glows expressing its heat.
A voice it speaks into my ear,
Saying, 'I'll tell you a secret if you buy me a beer.'

'Tell me! Tell me!' I beg at my knees.
This is a joke, a blatant tease!
Then I hear it, a whispering mutter.
'It's no joke, it's a serious matter.'

I listen carefully and take it in,
Then the voice disappears and the morning draws nigh,
The ghostly night has come to an end
And another night is just round the bend.

Peter Morris (13)
Homewood School & Sixth Form Centre

Inside My Head

Great minds,
Relaxing thoughts everywhere.
Everything is always the same
And always will be.
The whole world stays the same forever,
Motion and moves.
In the same worlds,
Nothing ever changes.
Dandelions and roses,
Smooth and gentle.

Matt Bridgeman (13)
Homewood School & Sixth Form Centre

Great Minds

Minds are great,
They think so aloud,
They say good things,
And make me proud.

A great mind I know,
Belongs to my grandad,
Who can answer any question as he would know.

His mind is old,
So full and so true,
Yet bold and old,
Yet through and not blue.

Grandad's mind is clever and quick
Which means he is able to still play a trick
It's full of knowledge, his mind I know
It's full of love that I won't let go.

Charlotte Houps (12)
Homewood School & Sixth Form Centre

Great Minds

My mind is a dancer jump-kicking across the studio.
As she flips into a hop-bull change,
The flick-bull change stores my secrets
Like an unlocked diary.
My memory is a kick-flip replaying constantly.
At the front of my mind is a mid-air flip
For a very important exam I have to pass.
The freshest thing in my mind is a new dance routine.

My dream for my great mind is
For it to be remembering professional dancers' dances.
The blood rushing through my brain
Keeps my feet moving to the beat.

Sophie Oliver (13)
Homewood School & Sixth Form Centre

Great Minds

He won't dare give up, not a chance,
Trust me, he'll find a way out.
He will focus on nothing more
Than the task that has been given.
Nothing can disturb him,
Not even the smallest word.
He's being tactical, dodging every error.
Speeding through seconds . . .
He's now halfway there, not a single error.
An objective needed and he will finish.
No chance to stand and chat as seconds whizz by.
He needs to finish his masterpiece or he won't get a good grade.
He won't, he can't give up.
As he is almost finished, and time is tight.
He must stay focused on what to do.
Ten minutes gone, five minutes left,
Scribbling along; finished now. Guess what?
He's *me!*

Jack Mounstephen (11)
Homewood School & Sixth Form Centre

Inside My Head

Inside my head is a complex maze,
I take turns which are right,
I take turns which are wrong,
Sometimes I am puzzled what turn to go to.
My mind is an imagination,
I think of lots of things,
What am I going to be like when I am older?
What is my life going to be like?
What other things will I discover?
Inside my head, I wonder . . .

Louise King (12)
Homewood School & Sixth Form Centre

Wayne Rooney

His mind has focus,
He's determined and never gives up
And always fights for the ball,
He has a lot of stamina,
He has a lot of confidence on the ball
And always takes on the hardest player
On the pitch even if it's Thierry Henry,
Roberto Carlos and Patrick Viera
Who are the best players in the world.
I am committed to my school work and football,
I am very determined to achieve the grade
I want in my school work,
I am self-disciplined to not hit my sister
When she hits me when I am watching TV
And then I go and talk to my mum and dad about it.
If I had a trial for the England team I would make it
But I do not know which team I would get in;
A, b, c, d, I believe that I would get into the c team for
England for the under 12s,
I would play in midfield or be the goalkeeper.

Dominic Roome (11)
Homewood School & Sixth Form Centre

Great Minds

My mind is a secret diary,
Thoughts all over my special place.
Memories and memories written down
And locked away in the back of my head,
Things that I will never forget!
My great mind taking in millions of new things
Which I learn every day.
Remember to lock your mind away,
Throw away the key and rest it
Ready for the next day!

Michelle Rogers (12)
Homewood School & Sixth Form Centre

Great Minds

She thinks so much about her job,
She has to practise so much,
She earns so much money,
She is a true star.

Her mind has a target,
I am sure she will succeed,
She will never give up,
She is mega rich.

Her fame has led to money,
Money has led to fame,
She is on TV quite a lot,
She has sold so many albums.

Her music is great,
So is her well-tuned voice,
She's so good live,
She never goes wrong.

She is a beautiful woman
With a beautiful voice,
Her beautiful voice
Makes her worth so much.

Kirstin Warnett (11)
Homewood School & Sixth Form Centre

Inside My Head

My mind is the god of all my body,
It stores all of my past and awaits my future,
Like my own control room, much like a computer.
It's hidden behind my eyes, a deeply blacked-out place.
It stores all of my memories in a big steel case.
It controls from my toes to my head.
It helps me figure out my schoolwork,
Even though I would much rather be in bed.

Harry Kelleher (12)
Homewood School & Sixth Form Centre

Inside My Head

Inside my head there's a thought or two,
Could I be the next Tiger Woods?
That would be a dream come true.
Sunny days, thunderstorms, sleet or snow,
Ice creams, umbrellas, a toboggan to show.
Money, fast cars and a chick on my arm,
Tractors, cattle, maybe a farm.
These are all thoughts, but they float round my head,
Turning to dreams when I take to my bed.
Helping old ladies to cross over the road,
Being a spy and learning the latest Morse code.
Christmas cards, carols and presents galore,
Discarded wrapping paper all over the floor.
I cannot believe how this information stays in my head,
Because that's only a fraction of thoughts I have said.
There's other data that's stored in my brain,
$3b + b + y$, it's all the same.
Cromwell, Henry and all of his wives,
Bunsens, gases, dissecting frogs with sharp knives.
Geography, English, ERS and IT,
Home economics, Welsh tea cake for me.
My dad said I should have called this something else instead,
He doesn't think I have much in my head.
'Vacant, to let, empty,' he joked
My dad he is quite a funny bloke.
The brain is the most amazing thing
Storing all thoughts and knowledge
Tied like a big ball of string.
All I have told, the things I have said,
These are just some of what goes on in my head.

Charlie Bedwell (12)
Homewood School & Sixth Form Centre

My Mind Is A . . .

Pink handbag,
It's full of lots of feelings and thoughts,
Pictures in my purse,
Diary thoughts.
My mind is a pink handbag,
It's filled with my most precious belongings,
A nice pink mirror,
A juicy red lolly.
My mind is a pink handbag,
It has a set of keys
To enter my house
Where most of my life is centred around.
My mind is a pink handbag.
In the middle of my pink bag,
My pink phone lays,
It's like a door opening up into my world
In many different ways.
The thoughts and feelings of my really kind mates,
The exciting dinner dates
I share with my mates,
And when I sit eating,
I sit there and think,
Who is going to take all the empty plates?
When we finish and step outside,
I wonder what my mind might think or find?

Emma Wakefield (12)
Homewood School & Sixth Form Centre

Great Minds

She is happy with what she gets,
She is tactical,
She is calm,
She never gives up,
She concentrates,
She gets high achievements.

Concentration is her key,
As well as her tactics and the crowd,
She gets high on the podium,
Smiling with joy and happiness,
Collecting her medal
For everyone to see.

Thinking of her next race,
Exercising and practising,
Thinking, *will I get another gold medal,*
Thinking of the day ahead.

When it's time to race
She warms up,
Thinking, *concentration is the key.*
When I race she is still concentrating,
When she has won,
She thinks, *well done Kelly Holmes!*

Scarlet Wilson (11)
Homewood School & Sixth Form Centre

The Most Scariest Place Is In Your Mind

My mind is a box of chocolates,
I can be sweet, like strawberry cream,
Or mean, like the darkest chocolate
That I've ever seen.
My worries are darkness lurking beneath my bed,
My nightmares still haunt me,
This I still dread.

Sean Weekes (12)
Homewood School & Sixth Form Centre

Great Minds

He has amazing focus,
He is determined to get the ball,
He always plays fair and tactical,
He always puts his body through hell,
His mind is always on the job.

He does not care what time he has to get up to train,
Cristiarno Ronaldo is committed to playing football,
He is keen on playing football,
He makes sure that he never lets the ball go without a fight,
He makes so many chances.

He never gives up even if it seems hopeless,
He always gives people an even chance,
He spends a lot of time on his hair,
He plays football on the Portugal and Man U teams,
He played at the 2004 Olympics.

He changes his football boots every match,
He always plays by the rules.

Jake Wilson (11)
Homewood School & Sixth Form Centre

My Mind

My mind is a confused child,
I don't know what's happening around me,
And I don't know what to do.
My mind is full of useless images and words,
It is so horrible, when I want to concentrate
The dark inside my head
Is overtaking the good and light.
But by concentrating on this poem
I have revealed the good and light
Inside my head.

Thomas Reeves (12)
Homewood School & Sixth Form Centre

My Mind Is A . . .

My mind is a word search,
I don't know how to say anything,
It's all muddled up, like scrambled egg,
I spell things backwards, but I don't know what,
Everything I think of, it's never right,
But saying that, I'm not very bright.

And now my mind is spaghetti Bolognese,
It's all lumpy and bumpy,
Also twisted like a rope.
It's lovely with bread, it's all dull and smooth,
It's hard to think inside my brain,
That's why I don't know my name.

Lee Rathbone (12)
Homewood School & Sixth Form Centre

Inside My Mind

My mind is a warm bath bubble full of worries.
There are warm bubbles popping all the time,
See-through and large, always more every day,
Getting bigger and bigger.
Every time the bubbles have a different thought in them,
Worrying about tests, GCSEs, jobs.
Always changing.
Changing every day, eventually they pop and go,
New ones come again, this time different ideas in them.
They come and go, school, friends, clothes, family,
These are all ideas inside my mind.

Adèle Purvis (13)
Homewood School & Sixth Form Centre

My Mind Is . . .

My mind is a man with a TV remote,
But I'm the TV.
I can never make up my mind,
I can never be me.
My mind is my shoes,
They change all the time,
People say it's OK,
And it's not a crime.
My mind is a computer,
Saved into a memory,
And it goes on forever,
Back into the century.

Lauren Waring (13)
Homewood School & Sixth Form Centre

Great Minds

G ood imagination always helps
R ight thoughts pop in and out
E xcellent work gets you good grades
A friend who helps makes it easier every day
T imed work is slightly hard.

M oney doesn't buy you the job you want
I gnorance won't get you anywhere
N o one cares unless you're there
D one all the hard work that you can
S o it's up to you what you do right now.

Alysa Virani (12)
Homewood School & Sixth Form Centre

My Mind

My mind is like a jail cell, 12" by 4",
White all round.
I sit in a straight jacket,
My thoughts can't escape,
They are always trying to get out.
The key to my thoughts is never to be found.

My mind is a shoelace,
A coiled rope, just like a snake.
It tries to slither around,
Shedding its skin just like my thoughts.
The snake is out of control,
Slithering fast, bashing all corners,
Trying to get away.

Robert Kirby (13)
Homewood School & Sixth Form Centre

Great Minds

My friend Glyn has a great mind,
He uses his great mind and
He's so determined!
Glyn helps me a lot
When I'm feeling blue
And don't know what to do.
Glyn's mind is always switched on
And when he's done
He never turns off his great mind
Until he finds that
He has helped others
With his great mind.
He's so tactical
And definitely practical
All because of his great mind!

Jade Pemberton (12)
Homewood School & Sixth Form Centre

Elvis Presley

Elvis was a legend
A hero and a saint
To many people
He inspired them to create
He starred in lots of films
And made many, many albums
His dancing was spectacular
And fans, he made thousands!
The King of rock 'n' roll
Was how he was best known
Gracelands was a mansion
And also his home!
He made loads of dollars
And had lots of followers
He died alone, in a place he called 'home'.

Sophie Kimber (11)
Homewood School & Sixth Form Centre

Great Minds Are *Sooo* Great!

G reat minds
R eflect on other people's minds
E veryone's mind is like a theme park, going
A round and around until you say, 'Great!'
T oday your mind is great, but tomorrow great minds
   Will be all around.

M inds are great
I nside you're wild
N aughty and cool
D aily make life worthwhile
S o just remember, great minds are great and so are you!

Matthew Savage (12)
Homewood School & Sixth Form Centre

Wayne Rooney

He's quick,
He's focused,
He has so much confidence.

He's so committed,
He so tactical,
He has so much co-ordination.

He always scores,
He never gives up,
He never even gives up when he has an injury.

His face isn't what made him famous,
That's for sure!
It's his feet and agility that help him to score!

He has so much determination,
So much no one can understand,
That's why he's at Man U!

Even if he doesn't get picked
He will always come back,
He won't let anyone take his place without a fight.

No one can ever be like him
Not even David Beckham.
Rooney just gets on with it, succeeding every game,
Every time, all the time!

Jack Ward (11)
Homewood School & Sixth Form Centre

Great Minds

My mind is a piece of twisted spaghetti,
Slimy and stringy, thin and long edges,
And minced beef in the middle, stringing all my ideas along,
Yellow and smooth, slithering like a snake through my teeth.
In my mind, the onions sizzle hot like a steamy bath.
The chilli powder burns inside me light a bright idea.

Charlie McKenzie (13)
Homewood School & Sixth Form Centre

Great Minds

His mind is set
On nothing but the ball,
He slowly lifts his head
Looking at the goal.

He runs in and out,
Getting near to the box
And he won't stop
Till he's got the goal.

He's got determination,
With that he can win
And using tactical skills
He can score.

Bang!
That's the sound of the ball
Hitting the net, his shot
Involved great concentration,
The name's Wayne Rooney.

Travis Paige (11)
Homewood School & Sixth Form Centre

Thomas Edison

His commitment runs through his veins and soul,
He combines his faith and intelligence to make one.
He has that discipline to try one more time.
His mind is set on achieving alone.
His belief in what he does is strong, stronger than iron.
His experience shows what he can do,
With or without any encouragement.
His expectations of his ability can take him that bit higher.
His talent will take him further.
His end result stuns the world, what will he do next?
Unpredictable is what he is.

Stephen Douco (11)
Homewood School & Sixth Form Centre

Melissa

She has an imaginary friend called Billy,
Who makes her look very silly.
When she gets in the pool, she acts so very cool.
When she gets home she goes straight to her room.

When she gets mad she goes off and plays with Billy,
But we don't mind because she is cute and cuddly.
But when she gets the hump with me I think I'll stay away,
But when she's happy, she's nice and kind.

She walks around the house waiting for something to happen,
But now she looks around corners watching every day.
Every time she goes to sleep, bubbles blow out of her mouth,
While she snores as loud as she can.

Then she has her breakfast while throwing it all over the chairs.
Then she stops and watches TV.
She sits in front of the fire eating some cheese
Then she starts to talk to herself.

She pulls out her toys and plays with Billy.
When her mum comes down she curls up and goes back to sleep.
While she dreams she starts to move about.
Then she wakes up again and plays with Pip, her dog.

She sits down and waits for her brothers and sisters to come home.
She sits down and watches her dad play pool.
Although her dad is very small
He likes to think of himself as very tall.

As he moves Melissa follows him.
But she scratches herself and rips her skin
As her dad moves back she screams extra loud
But he cleans her up as good as new.

Although she is only two she acts very bravely.

Glen Pryor (11)
Homewood School & Sixth Form Centre

David Beckham

He is self-disciplined and committed to his work.

He will go out to train to get fit for his matches
And he will train for about 3 hours a day
And then have a rest because he will be
Very tired so he has a very long rest.
If it is raining he will still
Train because he wants to get fit.
He will be the best player on England's
Team because he trains hard in the morning
And there's no time for a cup of tea or coffee.
David trains hard so he can
Get into the team.
David will be the captain of the team because
He trains hard every single day.
David has been chosen the captain because
He can kick the ball very far
And he is very talented.
David has a wife who is called Victoria
And she is a pop star
And she sings very nice songs.
She does it in front of everybody
'Cause she is not afraid of anything going wrong.
David plays for England and their
Coach is Sven Goran Eriksson.
Sven has to shout at his team,
The defence cannot hear Sven because of the crowd.
David Beckham is the best.
David takes the free kicks and the penalties.
The goals that David Beckham has scored are 43.

Ryan Cooper (11)
Homewood School & Sixth Form Centre

Great Minds

Arrows fly throughout the air,
But still he stands there brave and determined.
He will lead them on to battle,
Victory is his only option
Or else doomed they will be.

He uses his clever and cunning plans to win the day,
Still he carries on the bloodshed,
Knowing most of his kinsmen are dead.

Reinforcements arrive, but they are no help,
He never gives up and he never will,
Even though all he sees is failure,
Until at last he wins the day.
Then and only then he will stop
But when will it be, that glorious moment?

When the last sword has struck its final blow,
Then and only then he can celebrate.
When he does it will be the biggest
And the best throughout the land.

Freddie Gibbs (11)
Homewood School & Sixth Form Centre

Great Minds

He's the best of all actors,
He was born to be a star,
He's rolling in money.
He may be shy
But . . . he's any girls
Kind of guy!
What a thriller he may be,
If you see him on the big screen TV.
Leonardo can't you see
You're the greatest actor there can be!

Charlotte Morris (11)
Homewood School & Sixth Form Centre

Joss Stone (A Great Mind)

She stands there tall,
Ready to sing,
Focused on her voice,
She's got her mind set on the fans,
She knows she can do it,
All the words swimming in her head,
Determined to do her best,
Going over and over the words in her mind,
Microphone clutched,
Rhythm of the music dances round her body,
Skin tingles,
Pulse races,
Beat takes her over,
Words and excitement jumbled together,
Separating words from thoughts,
She knows fans will love it,
Nothing to worry,
Give her best,
She does it,
It's over,
She gave it her all
And she succeeded.

Hannah Pau (11)
Homewood School & Sixth Form Centre

Royal Ascot Horses

Horses feet stamping on the ground,
Eagerly trying to win the race.
Jockeys standing up whipping them,
The crowd cheering for their horse to win
So they get their money.
All of the horses' muscles standing right out
As they go whizzing by,
Then the horn goes to say which horse has won.

Simone Wilson (11)
Homewood School & Sixth Form Centre

Enzo Ferrari

His brain was full of designs for amazing cars with amazing speed.
He began a revolution of 200mph cars,
He had an amazing mind for design
And never gave up when it was wrong.
His name is Enzo, that's a cool name!
He invented the *Ferrari!*
He decided to paint his cars *red!*
Wow, they are luxury cars.
Big engines propel the cars to 200mph.
He is my hero,
But sadly he is gone.
He passed away 11 years ago,
But, the legend still lives on.
With the: Ferrari Enzo,
550 Maranello,
612 Scaglietti and
360 Modena.

David Housman (11)
Homewood School & Sixth Form Centre

My Summer Holiday Poem

Right on the lovely, hot, sunny beach,
The pure white sand crunches under your feet,
You can taste fresh grapes, pineapples, oranges and a peach.
As you're swimming in the glistening, blue sea,
Other people on the exotic beach
Are enjoying their perfect cup of tea.
As I am drinking my favourite drink on the beautiful beach,
The colour of my drink I am drinking is tropical pink.

Elspeth Brown (11)
Homewood School & Sixth Form Centre

The Bunny Rabbit

Sitting in the garden
Laying on the grass,
Eating all the flowers,
Drinking its water.

Fluffy and friendly,
Wouldn't harm a thing,
White as snow and floppy ears.

Twitching nose, wiggling whiskers,
Slowly he starts to go to sleep.

So now, as you can see,
It must be a lovely,
Cute, white rabbit!

Kim Smith (12)
Homewood School & Sixth Form Centre

Great Minds

Inside, my mind is full of wonderful things,
Things that no one will never know
Like my own hidden garden buried deep underground.
No one knows it's there but me and my mind
And every time I get a new memory it's stored as a plant,
So it can never be destroyed,
They will live forever even when I die.
Your mind can hold anything you wish,
From dreams and worries to your future,
Only you will know, just you and your mind.

Chantelle Wood (12)
Homewood School & Sixth Form Centre

The Mind Of Champion Eventer Pippa Funnell

Pippa is an eventer,
Flying around the fences.
Her horses read her mind,
They never take risks.

Only once has she made a mistake,
With a horseshoe through her arm.
But that did not stop her,
She just hopped back on.

She is the world champion eventer,
Nobody has beaten her yet.
Her best horse is Supreme Rock,
He is seventeen hands and bigger than she.

Her resilience is amazing,
She always keeps her cool.
Determination is her master
And she is nobody's fool.

Emma Giles (11)
Homewood School & Sixth Form Centre

Great Minds

G reat thoughts,
R unning through my head,
E xciting things happening,
A gain and again,
T hen before you know it,

M agical things start to happen,
I mportant as they may be,
N ot to anyone else but myself,
D reams do come true,
S o be sure to believe in yourself!

Kayleigh Hesmer (12)
Homewood School & Sixth Form Centre

Great Minds

Wally Lee has a very good sense of humour,
He is really brave, also he's full of confidence,
He has a mighty strong mind
So he takes everything as a joke.

His funny mind is under his short, black spiky hair,
His eyes are very light blue,
They sparkle in the sunlight.

He has loads of mates and friends,
That shows that he is a very good friend,
But his sense of humour always gets them.

This man is a builder but he does a very good job,
He works very quick and fast.
Used to call him Wall.

Harry Sedden (11)
Homewood School & Sixth Form Centre

Great Minds

G reat minds
R unning through my head,
E lecting a memory
A nd nothing changes,
T ime and feelings remain.

M y life is getting shorter,
I 'm feeling the pain which is
N ever a shame,
D ying or not,
S urviving is at a cost.

Jonathan Penney (12)
Homewood School & Sixth Form Centre

Great Minds

He weaves through the players,
Focused on the ball,
His tactical skills will move
Him closer to achievement.

He keeps his head up
And gets past the
Players and goes for
The cross.

His determination can
Take him to the
Top, make him
The best.

When he's set
On the ball he might
Pass it, cross it or
Get it into the net.

Eddie Warne (11)
Homewood School & Sixth Form Centre

Wayne Rooney

He was training every morning,
He was tired at night,
He was ready for that cup,
That was coming right up.
His team was ready and proud,
He works from daylight to dark,
He runs up and down the field,
To try and get the football in the goal,
If they win or lose they are still proud.

Robert Tompsett (11)
Homewood School & Sixth Form Centre

Great Minds

A long white beard,
Large round glasses perched on his nose.
A long red coat
With shiny black boots.
Flying through the sky,
Pulled by large creatures,
One with a bright red nose.
He spends all year wrapping and sorting gifts
For all people on Earth.
He's helping people remember to give and share,
Making sure that we have the same at Christmastime.
He is helping us to remember the baby born in the stable.
Whether you are rich or poor, young or poor,
He doesn't forget a single sale.

Katie Dean (11)
Homewood School & Sixth Form Centre

Great Minds

His mind is set
On the task ahead.
His mind is confident
That he will achieve.
His mind is trained
So he can play.
His mind was blank
But now is full.
He weaves through the players
Like they're planks of wood.
His feet are like fire
Burning through the field.
His mind has worked out where to shoot,
Bang! it's in again.

James Richards (11)
Homewood School & Sixth Form Centre

Great Minds - Jo Jo

She's got a good voice,
She's talented,
She's well trained,
She's sold lots of tracks,
She's disciplined,
She's got great ambition,
She will do well . . .
Her mind is creative,
Her thoughts are fantastic,
Her movements are great,
Her songs are excellent,
Her mind is trained,
Her mind is focused,
Her thoughts follow her everywhere,
She will do well . . .

Emma Wink (12)
Homewood School & Sixth Form Centre

Whitney Houston

Her voice is strong
So that she can achieve her ambition.
Her voice runs through her body
Making her confidence grow.

She uses her mind,
A mind full of imagination
To achieve a song
To sing to the world.

When she sings her whole life depends on her,
Her focus is full,
She concentrates on the words,
The words that come from her mouth,
So she can succeed
In later life and become a real true star.

Ashleigh Britten (11)
Homewood School & Sixth Form Centre

Great Minds - My Mum

My mum is determined
To finish the job.
She'll work all night if she has to
And she'll never, never cry.

My mum is committed,
She'll be out of bed before you know it.
She keeps us all in tip-top shape
Until she's ill, then it's my turn.

My mum is friendly,
She's loving and carefree.
She's clever and good to help with homework
But best of all she's always there for me.

My mum's confident,
She'll try her best.
She persuades me
To have a go and not to be afraid.

My mum's supermum,
She'll take me to clubs.
She'll never complain
And doesn't make a fuss.

My mum has a great mind,
She can't use a computer,
But she's learning to
And that's my mum.

Alisha Styles (11)
Homewood School & Sixth Form Centre

Great Minds!

Chris Dryland has a determined mind,
The loving, brave, happy mind.
He's always full of confident thoughts,
With a super-strong resilience
And an enormous source of commitment.

His mighty mind is place beneath a layer of
Thick, spiky brown hair, with shiny eyes in front,
His spikes always let people know that he's got
A good, strong brain underneath.

That grand, old brain of his, is full of excitement,
Friendship and determination to do his best.
His mind is also full of love and happiness
And a touch of self-proving desire in there too.

Chris has a loving heart and a good, old brain
In his spike-haired head.
When you are with him, in friendship, you will bind,
But what I always say is Chris is full of great minds!

Emily Hodgson (11)
Homewood School & Sixth Form Centre

My Poem

He's a good football player,
He's self-disciplined,
He has his mind on the job.

He's committed,
He's the second captain,
He is good at his job.

He's disciplined,
He's great,
He is going to be in the next World Cup.

Emma Rye (11)
Homewood School & Sixth Form Centre

The Great Rooney Mind

He gets up every morning
To train well and hard.
His skill runs through his body,
He always has self-control.
A determined mind to achieve.

He represents his country,
Proud to wear an England shirt.
Everyone supporting him
And cheering when he scores.
He used to play for Everton
But got bought by Man Utd.
A talent so young
That you can't believe
He will succeed,
His name is Wayne Rooney.

David Dyer (11)
Homewood School & Sixth Form Centre

Elephants

Kind, friendly *elephants* with their skins so rough,
Horrible, nasty hunters who think they're really tough.

'Kill, kill,' the hunters chant,
Could you kill? I know I can't!

Kind, friendly *elephants* with their ivory tusks so white,
Horrible, nasty hunters who kill with all their might.

'Kill, kill,' the hunters chant,
Could you kill? I know I can't!

Poor, helpless *elephants,* they crash to the floor
Horrible, heartless hunters love killing more and more.

'Kill, kill,' the hunters chant,
Could you kill? I know I can't!

Stacey Roe (11)
The Sittingbourne Community College

Tulip
(Inspired by 'The Tulip Touch' by Anne Fine)

Clever and cunning,
Her eyes as cold as ice,
As she scurries away from danger,
Like 100 little, white mice.

Natalie and Tulip,
Always playing their naughty games,
Messing around in other's houses,
Then slipping down those getaway lanes.

Getting into trouble,
Is what Tulip likes best,
While sometimes the innocent little angel,
Fools all the rest.

Tulip storms down the street.
With a face full of thunder,
Is she OK? Is she really my friend?
Natalie did wonder.

Spending all her time at the palace,
With Natalie and her brother,
Not at home where she should be,
With her own father and mother.

Penny Seymour (12)
The Sittingbourne Community College

The Houghten Household

In the Houghten household there are dogs barking.
In the Houghten household there are computers whizzing.
In the Houghten household there is always something happening.

In the Houghten household there are TVs chattering and buzzing.
In the Houghten household there is water gushing and running.
In the Houghten household there is always . . . something happening!

Matthew Houghten (11)
The Sittingbourne Community College

The Funeral

Last week I went to a funeral,
I felt really sad
Everybody was dressed in black
And my mum felt really mad.

I had to bury my grandad's ashes,
Right under his favourite tree
My family were all crying
But crying isn't for me.

The day passed really quickly,
I didn't want to go home
I wanted to stay with my grandad
That's when the tears came.

I came home the next day
Went straight to my room
I knew my grandad would still be with me
Everywhere in my home.

Kim McDermott (11)
The Sittingbourne Community College

Hurt No Living Thing

Hurt no living thing,
      Ladybird, nor butterfly,
Nor moth with dusty wing,
      Nor cricket chirping cheerily,
Nor grasshopper, so light of leap,
      Nor dancing gnat,
Nor beetle fat
      No harmless worms that creep,
Nor ants that do march.

Amy Freeman (11)
The Sittingbourne Community College

Secondary School

S econdary school
E xciting and
C ool
O thers are helpful and kind
N othing really to be scared of
'D o your best' is the main rule
A fter school clubs
R ooms, rooms, lots of rooms
Y ou can go to an after school homework club at the LRC

S chool is normal
C old in winter
H ot in summer
O ther friends meet
O ther lessons you have never done before
L ong days at secondary school.

Jessica Eldridge (11)
The Sittingbourne Community College

Winter's Coming

All the children playing in the snow,
Making snowmen and having snowball fights.
Every single little child getting excited because
Christmas is coming. Presents to get, hoping it will snow,
Hoping it will be a white Christmas and having lots of fun.

All the days getting shorter, all the clocks turning back.
Parents getting miserable and moany, kids getting excited and happy.
The children making different sized snowmen
Which are melting as the sun comes up.
Throwing snowballs and missing each other
And making footprints in the snow.

Amy Webb (11)
The Sittingbourne Community College

The Tulip Touch
(Inspired by 'The Tulip Touch' by Anne Fine)

Tulip, Tulip tells a lie,
Hair is tangled, evil eye
Darkest hair
On darkest night
Tulip's mother gives a fright.

Tulip's games 'fat and loud'
'Road of bones' without sound
Tattered trousers, worn-out coat
Her clothes, the colour of a goat,
She lets a rabbit out its hutch
And puts poor Jeffrey in a crutch.

She loves the palace
Filled with dust
And always fills, we must, we must
Fire burning in Tulip's eyes
Fakes a smile, puts on a disguise
Tulip's father whips his dog
Her mother's jumping like a frog.

Tulip and Natalie
Till the end, will this friendship ever end?

Matthew Hendry (12)
The Sittingbourne Community College

Giant Tortoise

A slow eater
An ancient creature
A steady walker
A 200-year-old
An armoured tank,
A veggie eater,
An excellent crawler,
A brilliant walker.

Charlie Rochester (11)
The Sittingbourne Community College

The Tulip Touch
(Inspired by 'The Tulip Touch' by Anne Fine)

The Earth stayed well away,
Her eyes were on fire.
Tulip's home was like a scrapyard,
Life wasn't fair to her.

Her punches made a throbbing noise,
Her games will swallow you whole.
The terrible Tulip lies with detail,
Life wasn't fair to her.

Tulip walks like a punk,
Tulip is an evil girl.
Natalie is her puppet and friend,
Life wasn't fair to her.

Her mum, a timid cockroach,
Tulip, a devil child.
Her dad, a nasty bully,
Life wasn't fair to her.

She makes people cry,
Her heart's burning fierce,
She is polite to Natalie's mum,
Life wasn't fair to her.

Her new school's slimy green,
She lives a secret life.
She worships a fire god,
Life wasn't fair to her.

She is very unpopular,
Tulip and Natalie were split up.
After school, they meet up,
Life wasn't fair to her.

Natalie is now on fire,
Like Tulip was before.
Her dad has a raging smile,
Life wasn't fair to her.

She swears foully at Natalie,
Natalie is now ignored.
Tulip is rude like a baboon,
Life wasn't fair to her.

She soaks up to Natalie's dad,
She loves the sight of fire.
The clouds were making an angry face,
Life wasn't fair to her.

She has a fake smile,
She sets difficult tasks.
She has certain darkness,
Life wasn't fair to her.

She will spread her unpopularity . . . *to you!*

Leon Gorman (13)
The Sittingbourne Community College

Sunset

S un sets over the ocean, lighting up the sky,
U nwelcome darkness spills over the land,
N ight draws in waiting to die,
S unrise in the morning,
E very inch of peaceful land covered in
T wilight, waiting to start all over again.

Alexandra Brookman (11)
The Sittingbourne Community College

Fudge

F udge is my fluffy cat
U nder his fur is a devil
D ogs at night terrorise the cat
G rey and brown is his fluffy fur
E ating his food every minute.

Jordan Houghton (11)
The Sittingbourne Community College

Tulip
(Inspired by 'The Tulip Touch' by Anne Fine)

Standing there a girl in white,
Like an angel on a summer's night.

The strange girl just standing there,
With her matted, ruffled, unbrushed hair.

Tulip was there, Tulip was fun,
Natalie thinks Tulip is number one.

Along came Tulip, along came pain,
Along came thunder, cloud and rain.

What a strange girl with her strange games,
And their strange, unusual names.

Now Tulip and Natalie both run wild,
Is Tulip a girl or a demon child.

Along came Tulip, along came pain,
Along came thunder, cloud and rain.

Zoe Tyler (13)
The Sittingbourne Community College

The Cheetah

The cheetah - a deadly killer
The ultimate hunter
Runs faster than the wind can blow
Glides like a feather in the wind
Every step you take he's watching you
Claws as sharp as a jagged rock
Sits there waiting for its prey
The cheetah reminds us of the real killer.

Guy Cornelius (11)
The Sittingbourne Community College

Tulip
(Inspired by 'The Tulip Touch' by Anne Fine)

Tulip hurried along the path splashing and squelching
through puddles.
Her sad and lonely face was like the dark, misty sky above her.
She looked terrible like she had been dragged through dirty piles
Of mud and grass with her cheap shoes and tatty clothes.

Tulip is like a small sneaky cat when playing her games
But like a little child at Christmas time,
Messing about with toys.

Hurting people's feelings is what Tulip does best.
Laughing at people and making them cry.
Like walking terror who everyone avoids.

Tulip seems like an onion with layers as there are may different
sides to Tulip.
How unfortunate for people who cross her path.

Hollie Parkinson
The Sittingbourne Community College

Tulip Poem
(Inspired by 'The Tulip Touch' by Anne Fine)

Here comes Tulip,
Here comes the Devil,
Here comes the destruction of the Earth.
Oh, this person is a devil in disguise,

Natalie's dad, what a silly person believing that Tulip is a nice person.
What about poor Julius? Such a shame he is hurt too.
Even though Natalie noticed Tulip's nastiness,
Tulip doesn't like Natalie but why? Why?
Natalie's mum thinks the same as Natalie,
This Tulip is like an angel but deep down,
Oh what destruction.

Nathan Bibbings (13)
The Sittingbourne Community College

The Tulip Touch
(Inspired by 'The Tulip Touch' by Anne Fine)

Thump! Thump! Thump! Here comes Tulip
With her unbrushed hair and cheap clothes she's like a dustbin
　　　　　　　　　　　　　　　　　　　　　　　on legs
The stupid games and awful lies are just a few things that she does
She tricks us, she teases us, she torments and tortures us.
All because her dad threatens her!

In the class she annoys us
Even when we are on the bus
I swear her heart is a black hole
When she does nasty things she's like,
'Oh, look at me I'm on a role!'
And when the bell goes for class
She screams as if to break the glass.

All her time is spent at the palace
Where she always shows signs of malice
She gets worse and worse
Next she'll be stealing somebody's purse!
She plays nasty tricks
Then hides behind a pile of bricks
As not to get caught
Her score against us is a million to nought.

I wonder what her feelings are like
Deep down inside . . .
Is it evil or is it sad?
You can never tell.
Could she be thinking up evil thoughts
Or wondering why we hate her?
But there's always one answer . .
And that is . . . she's always going to be the same old Tulip.

Jodie Shepherd (13)
The Sittingbourne Community College

Tulip And Natalie
(Inspired by 'The Tulip Touch' by Anne Fine)

Tulip and Natalie, two peas in a pod
Then the Devil rose and floods began.
Each one hurt
One way or another.

Tulip feels she has everything wrapped
round her pinkie
But Natalie knows her like the back of her hand.

Tulip's stupid games of such nonsense
Will push her luck
And trouble will soon find its way.
For people will anger
With torment she plays
With Natalie, and the stupid games.

For Tulip, Christmas with Nat was great delight
As she'd get what she wanted
Without putting up a fight.
She would flirt with Nat's father,
Be polite to Nat's mum,
All to be loved and get food in her tum.

Natalie, a face of innocence,
Such as an angel.
Tulip, her eyes filled with fiery flames from the depths of Hell.
Tulip and Natalie,
Two peas in a pod.
Then the Devil rose and floods began.

Emma Warren (13)
The Sittingbourne Community College

Tulip
(Inspired by 'The Tulip Touch' by Anne Fine)

I don't know why Tulip has her name,
For everything she does I get the blame.
For a tulip is a pretty brightly-coloured flower,
Not like our Tulip who thrives on power.

Tulip is a mystery, her mind a tangled web,
Of feelings and thoughts, everything that enters her head.
I don't think she's human, she never feels bad,
When she tricks or lies, or makes someone sad.
When she's angry, she's a raging storm,
Lightning, hail and thunder all in human form.

Her childish fits are a bit hard to take,
And sometimes of Tulip you need a break.
It's like she disappears into thin air,
You'll see her for weeks, and then she's not there.
She comes across tough, as hard as a rock,
But inside she's marshmallow, she's surprisingly soft.
Her dad is a bully, her house is a mess
So Tulip goes to the palace and tries to forget.

She lives two lives, one good, one bad,
And for Tulip, I feel quite sad.
Tormented by fear, but she doesn't let is show,
People could help her, if she'd only let them know.
She's not the toughest kid on the block,
And to Tulip that may come as a shock!

Sophie Deacon (12)
The Sittingbourne Community College

Who Is Tulip?
(Inspired by 'The Tulip Touch' by Anne Fine)

Who is Tulip?
Bottled up and brutal.
Trying to escape her cage like a cat on its way to the vets.
Her clothes, tattered and torn.
As she lies her life away.

Tulip's behaviour, disobedient and disruptive,
With her comments, hurtful and harmful.
Laughing and playing jokes on people
As she lies her life away.

Tulip's game's good for two, bad for one.
Always Natalie the told off one
Her dad's threats into games
As she lies her life away.

As Tulip enters the palace Natalie's dad is wrapped,
around her little finger.
In the palace she plays all day.
With her eyes a-gaze on the world.
As she lies her life away.

Looking to the future.
What will we see?
More of the same
Or will she change?
That's Tulip!

Jodie Roberts (12)
The Sittingbourne Community College

Fish Fingers

At the Sea Life Centre
I see fish scales . . .

Fish fins . . .
But I didn't see any
Fish fingers!

Mitchel Platt (13)
The Thomas Aveling School

A Meal For A Hawk

A hawk is silent in a tree
Sitting in silence, not a word
Staring down below.

In his sight the hawk sees
A supper in the making
The hawk is clever
The human's not.

The hawk with its belly rumbling
And saliva dripping from its mouth
Sees the boy playing
Playing with his rabbit.

The boy goes in
Now's the chance
The hawk swoops down
And grabs the rabbit
All that's left is a feather!

David Colbourne (11)
The Thomas Aveling School

What Miss?

We ran out of dog food
And Mum gave the books to my dog!
I ran out of paper doing my other homework.
My pen ran out and I didn't have a spare!
I must have dropped it on the way to school.
Sorry Miss.

It must be in my locker
And my keys are at home.

Er, I forgot Miss!

Taylor Grindley (12)
The Thomas Aveling School

Darkness

Darkness comes,
Stars come out
Owls hoot from somewhere in the distance
That's when you start to hear
Strange noises,
From the heart of the forest.

The hairs on the back of your neck
Stand up in fear.
You look around
But no one's there.

Crack!
A stick breaks
You look around for the culprit . . .
Then realise, it's just you.

Sophie Baldock (12)
The Thomas Aveling School

Cat

Purr maker
Furry raker

Bird's surpise
Laser eyes

Whisker tickler
Milky licker

Fish eater
Bird killer

Light sleeper
Centre feature

Licks its fur
It's a her.

Soren Sutton (12)
The Thomas Aveling School

Guinea Pig

Carrot eater
Light sleeper

Fat lump
Hairy clump

Lawn mower
Hay thrower

Cuddle taker
Fuss maker

Strong bite
Cute sight

Finger licker
Food flicker

Good hider
Even kinder

Fast drinker
Quick thinker

Attention seeking
A lot of peeking
Little pig
Not that big.

Jennifer Taylor & Joanne Peterson (12)
The Thomas Aveling School

The Sun Is . . .

The sun is shiny
On a hot summer's day.
We burn like bacon
On a hot summer's day.
We like to play
On a hot summer's day.
It floats on a blue carpet
On a hot summer's day.

Hannah Wallington (11)
The Thomas Aveling School

I Don't Want To Go To School Mum
(Inspired by 'I Don't Want To Go To School Mum' by Pam Ayres)

I don't want you to go to school Son!
We are going to go shopping Son
I thought you liked going shopping Son
We're going to get a lot of stuff Son
And you're going to carry a lot of stuff Son
I am going to make you go and get everything Son
I might even tell you to do everyone else's shopping Son.

I will start a business Son
You will work all day and night Son
You won't be able to sleep Son
You won't be able to play with your toys or even go to bed Son
I'll be rich Son and you will sleep in the cellar
We will be there soon Son you'd better get ready.

Oh looks there's your school Son
You won't be going in there Son
'Bye Mum, I'm going to school
I don't want to work for life, bye Mum.'
I knew that would get him.

Aaron de Bruin (11)
The Thomas Aveling School

The Sun Is . . .

A golden fireball
A searchlight watching over the world.

A lion's mane
A candle burning away as night falls.

The Olympic torch
The stars' street lamp guiding them through the universe
A sea of fire
A yellow lollipop lighting up your tongue.

Matthew Jeffreys (11)
The Thomas Aveling School

Bang! The Football Poem

Bang!
I fall to the ground,
The intensity is shaking in the ground,
The ref blows the whistle,
He shouts, 'Free kick!'
I put the ball on the grass,
The crowd are moving very fast.

Then everything goes silent,
I hit it to the side,
The players shouted, 'Offside.'
The ball hits the bar,
The keeper goes to catch,
Slips over in a wet patch,
The ball goes in,
The crowd go - we win.

Tom Morgan (12)
The Thomas Aveling School

The Sun Is . . .

A giant golden chandelier
Flying high in the air,
A lion guarding the sky,
Roaring loudly and raging.

The sun is butter that is spread on the world.
The sun sizzles and burns.
Spaceman probably say,
'Do you want an English fry, way up by the sun?'

It is yolk, it is egg,
The Olympic torch of 2004,
It is anger that never burns away.

Lorna Fazakerley (11)
The Thomas Aveling School

My Ufter Dufter

My ufter dufter
Is black and white
My ufter dufter
Doesn't sleep at night.

My ufter dufter
Scares the pants of my mum
My ufter dufter
Has a bright pink bum.

My ufter dufter
Plays with the dog
My ufter dufter
Blocks up the bog.

My ufter dufter
Has big red eyes
My ufter dufter
Likes eating pies.

My ufter dufter
Is my imaginary friend
My ufter dufter
Drives me round the bend.

My ufter dufter
Has left with his case.

Beware! I think he's on your face!

Kirstin Bicker (11)
The Thomas Aveling School

Untitled

Mum brings out a tray of hot dogs
They really smell yummy.
I take one off, bring it to my mouth
I can't resist to take a bite.
They really taste scrummy
Like my heaven.

Lauren McLeod (11)
The Thomas Aveling School

Mouth-Watering Motionless Muffins

Three in each row,
Soft and delicate as a falling petal,
Cuffed so perfectly in each majestic case,
Outlining the dark golden outer edge,
The lightness in the centre - a golden beeswax colour,
Placed on a vibrant table, each row a different colour,
Each mouth-watering muffin so fresh,
As it rises in the oven, the fresh smell getting to me,
Making my stomach roar in hunger uncomfortably,
So yielding soft and cushiony, smooth and bumpy in places,
The temptation of their oven fresh, motionless pose,
Small, juicy blueberries positioned, immobile,
The oven fresh smell making my nostrils flare,
As they come out of the hot oven smelling so soft,
                                      so pure and innocent,
Waiting for me to bite into the supple textured sponge,
The first bite making me yearn for more,
The last bite filling me up, but I'm still craving more . . .

Sabrina Powar (14)
The Thomas Aveling School

Chilli Con Carne

I like chilli con carne,
Because it's spicy and special,
Like a day at the seaside.

I like the sauce,
Because it's hot and tasty,
Like hot rain water.

I like the beans,
Because they roll down my throat,
Like a football being kicked down the pitch.

I like the rice because it's plain and tasteless
Like water.

Johnathan Sutton (11)
The Thomas Aveling School

Sausages & Mash

M ash is creamy and yellow
A lways a delight to eat
S ausages and mash goes down with a bang
H ave back-up just in case.

&

S ausages are good for your tummy
A lso very yummy
U sually not lumpy
S oft sausages sizzling in a saucepan
A nd spurting out lots of fat
G oing down my throat
E asy to eat
S oon it's all over, I've got to get some more to eat.

Amy Dettmar (12)
The Thomas Aveling School

The Sun Is . . .

A lion, fierce
A candle burning
A golden coin
A ball of fire
A torch shining in the sky
A colour of orange and yellow
A fiery oven
A sizzly ball.

It's all around the world
Warm,
　　Hot,
　　　　Boiling.

Priyanka Mistry (12)
The Thomas Aveling School

Chilli Con Carne

Chilli con carne,
It's as good as a party,
It's spicy and special.

It's scrummy and yummy,
It's good for your tummy,
It's like . . . living in paradise.

Put in rice and some spice,
Now some sauce
(That's as pretty as a horse),
And you have the perfect main course!

Katie Harden (12)
The Thomas Aveling School

The Sun Is . . .

A golden coin,
A fiery ball which is not fun to play with,
A fierce lion with a golden mane,
A tiger like a torch in the dark,
A sea of fire, orange and yellow,
A million golden hairs as hot as a supernova,
A big fiery tail curled up in a ball,
A big searchlight searching all space,
A big shiny oven like a happy face on holiday.

Alexander Rossiter (11)
The Thomas Aveling School

Jelly

Jelly, cool like ice,
So fresh, so clear,
Pale, sliced strawberries fringed with seeds,
The texture of the jelly in my mouth,
As it slides down my throat.

Andreas Eliades (14)
The Thomas Aveling School

The Game

They started the game going 1-0 down
All the boys had a frown,
At last they scored a goal,
Time to take away the other team's soul.
It was half-time,
Everyone was fine.
They had a talk,
The adults walked.
They came back on the field,
When minutes made the match sealed.
6-1 up, minutes to go
The referee blows as the ball goes out for a throw.

John Williams (11)
The Thomas Aveling School

A Soldier On The Battlefield

Fear bubbling in the pit of my stomach,
The bombs have started to fall,
The explosions are deafening,
Gunfire cracks through the night,
Bullets skim through the air,
Adrenaline pumps through my veins,
Pushing away the fear and doubts.

Lizzie Cook (13)
The Thomas Aveling School

Strawberry Cheesecake

The sweet, subtle strawberries, bursting on my tongue,
So fresh, so neat, melting for so long,
The gentle, light, creamiest cream,
Floats on my tongue like a dream,
Raspberries, pink as a crimson lipgloss,
Embedded, trapped for extra juiciness.

Amandeep Thind (14)
The Thomas Aveling School

Sarah

My name is Sarah
I am three
My eyes are swollen
I cannot see.
I must be stupid
I must be bad
What else could have made
My daddy so mad?
I wish I was better
I wish I wasn't ugly
Then maybe my mummy
Would still want to hug me.
I can't speak at all
I can't do you wrong
Or else I'm locked up
All day long.
When I'm awake
I'm all alone
The house is dark
My folks aren't home.
When my mummy does come
I'll try and be nice
So maybe I'll get just
One whipping tonight.

Kuldeep Bahia (11)
The Thomas Aveling School

Mango

The sweet smell wafts over my nose,
It has a smooth feel,
One lovely taste,
I love it,
It's very yellow,
Lovely and yummy to eat.

Rosa Housby (12)
The Thomas Aveling School

Chocolate So Sweet

Crunchy crumbly biscuit,
Coated in chocolate, oh so sweet.

Making me so hungry,
I just wanna eat, eat, eat.

Small little fingers,
Four in one go,
Chocolate so creamy,
All laid in a row.

Which one should I choose?
The one that's big and crunchy?
The one that's small and creamy?
The one that makes me hungry?
I just don't know!

Sam Chapman (14)
The Thomas Aveling School

First Bomb, Last Bomb

Horror for the people who heard their first bomb,
Scared, shocked people, fighting for their lives,
Explosions and shootings thunder throughout the city,
Terrified parents search for their worried children,
You can hear the horror of sad people crying,
'Why are they doing this?
All we want is peace.'
Blood splattered everywhere by terrorists,
Dying victims scared to lose their troubled lives.
Soldiers marching step by step,
Horror for the innocent people who heard their . . . last bomb.

Daniel Reeves (14) & Rosie Parris (13)
The Thomas Aveling School

Two Different Worlds

Sad, that's how people feel inside,
Watching, listening and feeling the pain,
Running through the men, women and children,
Of two different worlds.

Children flee from the sound of bombs,
Explosions fill the air,
Horror, screaming in their ears,
And death in their eyes.

The men are sad and scared,
But keep a strong look on their faces,
They worry that they will never see their families,
Their hearts beat faster with panic,
It stops,
It goes dark.

Toni Carter (13)
The Thomas Aveling School

Cheetah

Lightning runner,
Like the Gunners,
Hunting mad,
Ultra-bad,
Spotty coat wearer,
Cub carer,
Mega killer,
Guts spiller,
Meat taker,
Mess maker.

He's a clever
Little fella.

Robert O'Leary & Craig Evans (12)
The Thomas Aveling School

Take A Cake

O lovely cake,
O lovely cake,
How tasty is it.
When it is baked,
Chocolate cake,
Is better than hake.
Lemon slice,
Is so nice,
When I eat muffins,
They turn into nothing.

Carrot cake is . . .
Horrible!

Sam Jorba (13)
The Thomas Aveling School

A Poem On Food

Golden chicken sprinkled with pepper,
White rice cools on my tongue,
Spring onion lumps as green as grass,
Lovely salted chicken and rice,
Cashew nuts as salty as my chips,
A beautiful light yellow bean sauce,
Now I'm gonna lick my plate clean.

Tom Wadhams (15)
The Thomas Aveling School

Mango

The yellow colour is the same as the sun,
It tastes like a cool breeze in your mouth,
It smells like an orange in disguise,
It is lighter than the air on the ground,
It is more exotic than Hawaii itself,
It is a smooth and tasty pebble.

Amy English (13)
The Thomas Aveling School

My Sunday Best

Lamb which splits apart when cooked, well done,
Swimming in a pool of mint sauce that flows down
Over your dinner,
Yorkshire puddings that go soggy as they swim in the gravy.
Potatoes steaming as they come out of the oven,
Peas that are like little green marbles on your plate,
And standing proud, right in the middle, is the stuffing,
A rock among the river of thick brown liquid.

Kane Hallett (15)
The Thomas Aveling School

Berry Tasty

Mouth-watering strawberries,
They are berry tasty,
The juice dripping everywhere,
I like them with sugar or with ice cream,
The taste, the smell, the colours.

The smell reminds me of summer,
The taste is just delicious,
And the colours look like they're smiling,
Tempting me to eat them.

Sophie Bell (14)
The Thomas Aveling School

Eel Poem

Fishy pieces of clear jelly,
Shiny chunks of eel belly,
Hold it in your fingers,
Gnaw on the bone.
Shake a bit of pepper,
A splash of vinegar,
London's finest!

Steven Sanders (15)
The Thomas Aveling School

Hungry?

A hot succulent burger
Mounted on a freshly made salad.

The salad is cool like an ocean breeze,
But the burger itself,
With a stream of sauce running through the middle,
Is steaming hot.

It sits on the plate,
Steaming away,
Waiting for a hungry person,
To gobble it down,
Like water into a whale's deep, dark throat.

Joe Swanborough (14)
The Thomas Aveling School

Plate A Pasta

The pasta, golden in colour,
Flecked with herbs,
The tomatoes are red as blood,
Melting to sweetness,
Pepperoni, floating in a sea of colour,
Crisp sesame seed breadsticks,
Snap with a crunch.

Robert Gosling (14)
The Thomas Aveling School

Spider

Spider, spider, where did you go?
Spider, spider say hello,
Are you afraid of me?
Yes or no.
I'm scared to death of you,
I hope you know!

Matthew Baldock (11)
The Thomas Aveling School

War Poem

As I sit in my hole,
Digging down as if I were a mole,
I start to look up,
But I absorb the bullets like water to a cup.
I see the sarge shoot,
Gets the enemy in the boot.
We all make way for the tank,
As it heads straight for the bank,
I get my binoculars out and have a gaze,
Then I see a really big blaze.
All of our soldiers go to have a glance,
And we see our friend Lance.
He takes his chance,
But it blows in advance,
And the end of poor old Lance.
Blood and gore,
Slashed up the door,
Out came the enemy to loot the remains,
But we shoot and come out of the drains,
It starts to tip down with rain,
I feel a very sick pain,
In my brain,
As I lie in the rain,
All of my worries have been washed down the drain.

Danny Keane (13)
The Thomas Aveling School

Fear

The death of quietness,
The screaming of the terrified hostages,
As the sound of shooting deafens me,
My fear is like ice running through my veins,
Blood splatters everywhere,
Shatters lives as the bullets hit them.

Jade Minchin (13)
The Thomas Aveling School

Hopeless

Reduced to rubble,
Once a home,
An old lady crying,
She's all alone,
Children, now orphans,
This situation is hopeless.

Soldiers limping,
You can see the fear,
Drowning in gases,
So scary, you can hear.

The fire spreads,
A huge, hot light,
Dreams cut in pieces,
A horrible sight.

The land is deserted,
People walk through the curse,
The country must build again,
They wish for a nurse.

Leanne Doust (13)
The Thomas Aveling School

War

The guns are firing madly,
The sound of horrified screams fill the air,
The faces of scared men ready to die,
Then the explosions stopped.
The war is over,
Foggy air, full of mist,
The battlefield full of broken dreams,
Bloody bodies fill the field,
Guards shout to see if anyone is alive.

Louie Shaw (13)
The Thomas Aveling School

Under The Ocean

Far beneath the ocean, there it lays
All I have dreamed of.
Seeing dolphins prancing, a shoal of fish gathering together,
Jellyfish looking for fish,
Starfish flat as pancakes on the ground.

It was like I was in a dream,
There was a kingdom I dreamed of going in,
Then dolphins singing - some in pain,
I wanted to help. Then I woke up in my bed.

Natasha Prendergast (13)
The Thomas Aveling School

Weather

It's a rainy day today,
I hear the whistling winds streak by,
Today it's stormy,
Twister destroying towers,
Loud as a hi-fi,
Full of dust,
Thunder cutting through houses,
Lightning strikes so frightening.

Sam Van Der Tak (12)
The Thomas Aveling School

The Dreadful Night

It's stormy at night with people in fright,
The gusts blow but with a flow,
The wind goes on its toes,
The hurricane turns in its burn,
The lightning brightens as it fights,
The zaps strike with no lapse,
The wind whistles like a cat that bristles.

Lewis Church (12)
The Thomas Aveling School

Stormy Weather

Stormy weather wrecking your mind,
Bangs like a car blowing up,
Roaring thunder explodes in your ears,
Striking lightning hits with first degree burns,
Thunder thuds like a fist in your face,
Screaming people run from death,
Whistling wind sounds like a ghost,
Winds so strong, knocking trees.

Steven Edney (12)
The Thomas Aveling School

Tornado

Tornado flying through the air,
Thundery and blundery,
Frightening lightning crying loud,
Screaming winds across the river,
Roaring gales,
Jumping frogs,
Going somewhere they should not go,
Twister.

Steven Stewart (12)
The Thomas Aveling School

Dark, Dark, Dark

T ortured screams from here to there,
H owling whistles in the air,
E erie eyes that seem to stare

D aunting shadows make me shudder,
A ll around me bangs and clutter,
R attle, rattle, in the bellowing black,
K itchen light goes on . . . it's no longer dark!

Charlotte Hayes (11)
The Thomas Aveling School

Unfair

What possesses people to do
Things that kill
And frighten me and you?

Terrorist attacks all over town
Knocking down towers,
Our houses are down.

People bring mess and destruction,
In their path,
People are scared of abduction.

No one can stop them,
Not even Mr Blair,
It is really, really unfair!

Lottie Elvin (13)
The Thomas Aveling School

Civil War

Civil war,
What's so civil about that?
All the bloodshed and tears.

I'm out there now,
Gunshots all around,
The enemy moves closer and closer,
Until . . . *boom!*
They attack.

They may be our enemy,
But they are still our fellow men,
Same country, same language,
Just a difference of opinion,
So we attack.

Joanne Cooke (14)
The Thomas Aveling School

War Poem

Marching up and down the trenches,
Half dead no escape,
Men with forgotten boots,
Helmets clashing one against each other.

Then suddenly there comes the sign,
Green smoke rising,
A river of green smoke rushing through the trenches,
No escape.

One soldier, not quick enough,
Tries running but there is
No escape,
Eventually hunted down by this green beast.

Dead!
No way out,
Nowhere to run or hide,
No escape, suicide in everyone's eyes,
No escape, only over the top,
We are just waiting,
No escape.

Chris O'Brien (13)
The Thomas Aveling School

The War Is Starting

Quick! Quick! The war is starting,
Here comes the army marching,
Weapons and guns,
Not such good fun,
People dying,
People crying,
Poppies lying
In fields.

Kim Dhami (13)
The Thomas Aveling School

Waiting For The Signal

Laying there, waiting with my gun,
Staring at the shining sun,
Waiting, waiting for the signal.

Bang! Bang! There it is,
Off we go into the building,
What is it that they are shielding?

Taliban behind the door,
Don't want to be here any more,
Please, please don't even go there!

Ryan Brimsted (13)
The Thomas Aveling School

The Smell Of Death

The smell of death is pungent in the air,
Blood is stained up the walls,
Gas fills the room, rushing upwards,
I run from the billowing gas,
Rushing between my feet.
A ricochet of bullets comes flying,
Through the windows and doors,
I fall to the floor and my heart goes to rest.

Alastair Hutton (13)
The Thomas Aveling School

War

There is blood all around,
The gunshots are getting me down,
They are going *boom, boom, boom*.
I can hear them in my bedroom,
I shed a lonely tear,
As I sit up here,
This is a war.

Frances Pyke (13)
The Thomas Aveling School

Innocent Feet

Innocent feet walking on the hopeless ground,
The people of the war trudging on,
Some knowing they're walking to their deaths,
But others blind to what fate has in store.
They come to the battleground,
And see the enemies' eyes.
The devil, sin looking back at them.

Blood! Blood in their eyes,
That's what they see looking back at them,
A sudden explosion,
The soldiers fall back.

Emma Humphrey (13)
The Thomas Aveling School

The Screaming Chip

There lay a chip upon my plate,
And it was screaming, 'No don't eat me!'
It called for its mum so I called for mine,
So it called me a wuss!
So I cut it in half,
I was so angry, I picked it up,
Then let it go . . .
Into my mouth, the screaming chip fell!

Kemsley Perry (12)
The Thomas Aveling School

Farm Fresh Fry Up

Friend eggs like sunshine on my plate
Bacon liked ploughed fields
Sausages like the tree trunks
By a river of sauce.

Sonny Whiting (16)
The Thomas Aveling School

The Brave Still Marching On

Barely walking,
Mostly limping,
Some injured,
Some bleeding,
Some dying,
Families crying.

The brave still marching on.

Bombs falling,
Chaos all around,
The dead,
The dying,
Families crying.

The brave still marching on.

People screaming,
Lives destroyed,
Dreams corrupted,
People sad,
Going mad.

The brave still marching on . . .

Priya Vadher (13)
The Thomas Aveling School

War

A distant thunder of the tanks,
A soldier's day is done,
As he goes back to his resting base,
He lays down his gun,
Bombs are blowing,
Death is near,
His face is full of fear.

Ruth Humphrey (13)
The Thomas Aveling School

In Response To Pam Ayres' Poem
(Inspired by 'I Don't Want To Go To School Mum' by Pam Ayres)

'I don't want to go to school Mum.'
'I want you to go to school son,
Because it's good education.'
'But! But!'
'No, you are going to school.'
'Oh why Mum?'
'Just get in the car!'
'No Mum, I just want to stay home!
Oh Mum I've got a headache.'
'Excuses, excuses, all the time.'
'Mum I mean it.'
'If you're sick at school, they will ring.'
'Mum, please, oh please!'
'Get out or I will drag you out!'
'Mum I've got an earache.'
'Well son you just had a headache.'
'It passed on Mum.'
'Get out right now!'
'No Mum.'
'I'll come round and get you.'
'OK I will.'
Ooooh
I put all that hard work in
And she said *no!*

Liam Bartlett (11)
The Thomas Aveling School

Strawberry

Strawberries ripe,
Juicy and sweet,
I can't wait till
My mouth and you meet.

Conor Mahoney (12)
The Thomas Aveling School

In Response Of Pam Ayres' Poem
(Inspired by 'I Don't Want To Go To School Mum' by Pam Ayres)

'I don't want you to go to school, son,
I want you to help me cook the dinner,
Can you stay with me?'

'But I don't want to stay here
With you Mum,
I want to see my friends.'

'But I will take you shopping,
To buy you a new toy,
Or a treat or two.'

'OK I will stay with you Mum!'

Shantel Jarrett (11)
The Thomas Aveling School

Cool And Fresh

Mouth-watering,
Drip, drip,
Juicy feeling,
Mmmm . . .
Big in size,
Wow,
Seeds inside,
Pick, pick,
Black seeds, brown seeds,
Big seeds, small seeds,
Red inside,
Green outside,
Fresh and cool,
Crunchy and tasty,
Lovely and smooth.

Arzumand Faheza Ali (12)
The Thomas Aveling School

Strawberries . . .

Sometimes sweet,
Sometimes sour,
Red and juicy, that's my colour,
Fresh and healthy,
Polka dot skin,
Heart-shaped fruit,
Eat them with anything.
You put them in a bowl with
Cream and sugar,
I love the taste of the after flavour,
Rub them on your teeth,
And it takes away the stains,
Pop them in my mouth,
And that will make my day.
Strawberries.

Katie Jago (12)
The Thomas Aveling School

Woof! Woof!

Droopy ears,
Long tears,
Woof! Woof!
Always dives
Also alive,
Woof! Woof!
Loves to run,
Likes sweet buns,
Woof! Woof!
Eats everything in sight,
Watch out kids he'll give you a fright!
Woof! Woof!

Jodie Fraser (12)
The Thomas Aveling School

Chocolate

Brown light
A tastebud delight
Velvet silk
Yum
Lovely cold
Lovely warm
It melts so fast
Yum
Dip it in a hot drink
Dip it in a cold
Bite it
Suck it
Yum
Crunch it
Munch it
Yum
I've had too much!
I'm going to burst!
Yum
Chocolate.

Levi Verrall (12)
The Thomas Aveling School

Christmas

On Christmas Day
We run and play.

We all get presents,
For dinner we have
Roast pheasant.

We have fruit cake,
Freshly baked.

Last of all the fairy lights,
Make me feel ever so free.

Mecheala Leigh Mills (12)
The Thomas Aveling School

Rabbit

Nose twitcher
Ear itcher
Carrot muncher
Lettuce cruncher
Hops along
Does no wrong
Fur's all fluffy
Tail's all puffy
Lives in a hutch
Doesn't do much
A bed of hay
That's where I lay
There's Dutch
Long-eared and wild
A perfect present for a child.

Paige Bicker (12)
The Thomas Aveling School

Dolphin

Ocean swimmer
Water shimmer
Swimming all day long
Speaking with a song
Greeting friends
Echo sends
Leaping high
Touching sky
Wave riding
Fin waving.

Silky blue skin
Swims towards the sunset.

Abbie Holmes (12)
The Thomas Aveling School

I Want You To Go To School Son!

I want you to go to school son,
We're already at the school gate now,
I want you to go to school son,
You're like a wolf at home that just likes to howl.

I want you to go to school son,
I need to get our dinner ready,
I want you to go to school son,
Because if I don't get the dinner ready,
Then we'll get thinner and thinner.

I want you to go to school son,
Or you'll be bored at home,
I want you to go to school soon,
Then you won't be at home alone.

Nicole Teo (11)
The Thomas Aveling School

Strawberries

They're red and juicy,
Fresh from the bags,
They're very healthy,
Not like fags.
Some are small,
Some are big,
Some are short
And some are tall.
Some are sweet
And some are sour,
So come on then,
And taste the power.

Vickie Busher (12)
The Thomas Aveling School

In Response To Pam Ayres' Poem
(Inspired by 'I Don't Want To Go To School Mum' by Pam Ayres)

'Don't go to school,
Bad Son, I don't care what you do Son,
You can stay at home all day,
I'll even let you run away,
You'll have no money to buy your favourite sweets,
It'll be great fun without any treats.

People will laugh and stare,
At your ugly hair,
You'll have lots of friends,
With the parked Mercedes Benz.

Or we could fly round the world,
Strapped in a boring old plane,
Even go shopping,
To the end of your days.'

'No Mum, I'll go to school Mum,
Please Mum, school is fun,
Work, lots of work, Mum,
Anything Mum please.'

'Fine I'll take you to school . . .

I knew that would work!'

Alfie Mason (11)
The Thomas Aveling School

Fish

The fishes swimming in the sea,
By the fishing rod,
One silly fishy,
Bit the bait,
He was cod!

Grace Barker (11)
The Thomas Aveling School

In Response To Pam Ayres' Poem
(Inspired by 'I Don't Want To Go To School Mum' by Pam Ayres)

'I want you to go to school son,
Please get out the car son,
I want you to go to school,
All your friends are waiting son,
I want you to go to school.

I want you to go and play son,
The pips will go son, just go OK,
Please son, I'm waiting,
Your friends are going, go son,
The day will go quickly son.

I want you to go to school son,
Please do, get out son,
Go OK, please I'll open the car door,
Get out the car you stupid boy.'
'OK, OK keep your hair on Mum! Bye.'

Katie Dodsworth (12)
The Thomas Aveling School

The Beach

Children play all day on the beach,
Sandcastles they make and they play in the sea,
Pebbles and stones,
Sands on their toes,
Ice cream they lick, will go on their nose,
For every day they go to the beach,
They get a ice cream for a treat,
They sit on the beach with their ice creams in hands,
Watching the sea,
It splashed on my knee,
We all went home and had some tea.

Emma North (13)
The Thomas Aveling School

In Response To Pam Ayres' Poem
(Inspired by 'I Don't Want To Go To School Mum' by Pam Ayres)

'I want you to go to school Son.'
'Nooo!'
'Yes, now here is your lunch Son, now go.'
'Please, no I want to play with my truck.'
'No get in the car now, Son.'
'No, what are you going to do about it?'
'I will throw you in the car.'

'No . . . we . . . oaw.'
'Let's go.'
'I want to stay at home Dad, please.'
'No, you make too much mess in the house.'
'Please I won't Dad.'
'You get on my nerves Son and you do!'

Sam Price (11)
The Thomas Aveling School

Beach

At the beach
Making sandcastles
And playing games
Having fun
In the sun.

The sand rustling through
My feet feeling soft
And bright like sun in morning light.

Eating ice cream
Feeling soft and cold.

As I look around
Seeing people on the ground
Lazing on the sunny beach.

Rahcemul Mumin (13)
The Thomas Aveling School

I Want You To Go To School Son
(In response to Pam Ayres' poem 'I Don't Want To Go To School Mum')

I want you to go to school Son,
And learn all there is to learn,
I want you to go to school Son
And become a scientist.
I want you to go to school Son,
Not turn the butter in the churn.

I want you to go to school Son,
And have a load of mates,
I want you to go to school Son
Not die of boredom on the settee,
I want you to go to school Son,
Not burn in the fires of death but live again
In happiness not with grief under your chest.

I don't want you to stay at home Son,
But live in a world of knowledge,
I don't want you to stay at home Son,
Because you are already in the way,
I don't want you to stay at home Son,
But be happy every day.

Kyle Rogers (11)
The Thomas Aveling School

I Want You To Go To School
(Inspired by 'I Don't Want To Go To School Mum' by Pam Ayres)

I want you to go to school Son,
Because all you do is talk,
I want you to go to school Son,
Because you get in the way when I walk.
I'm sure you'll enjoy it when you're there Son,
I know you're a good boy Son but you do make too much noise!

Bradley Shuter (11)
The Thomas Aveling School

The Haunted House

The haunted house
Is on my road,
No one stays, everyone goes,
Lights flicker through the night,
I look through the window,
It gives me a fright,
One day I thought, *I'll take a look,*
Instead of a doorknob, they had a hook,
The windows were smashed,
I peered through, dust splashed
On the floor,
So I went through the door,
I crept in up the stairs,
And in a fruit bowl, sat mouldy pears.
I went in the bedroom, cor what a smell.
I looked in the cupboard and there was a dead owl,
I ran as fast as I could,
I got to the door
There I stood,
I would have left,
But the door was stuck,
He's coming to get me . . .
Aarrgghh!

Kelsey Fordham (13)
The Thomas Aveling School

In Response To Christina Rosetti's Poem 'Sea, Sand And Sorrow'

What is light? Feathers and wheat,
What is shiny? Suns and moons,
What is long? Roads and trains,
What is blue? Skies and blue eyes.

Jennifer Cordingley (12)
The Thomas Aveling School

Dinner

'What do you want for dinner?
Fish? Yes, fish.'
'I don't like fish.'
'Yes you do.'
'Yes, fish and chips.'

'You're not having fish and chips.'
'Please!'
'No, have salad.'
'Don't like salad!'

'Fine go hungry.'
'Don't want to.'
'Get something to eat then.'
'Fine, I'll get fish.'

John Luke Fright (11)
The Thomas Aveling School

The School!

The school is a good place to learn,
Desks are all in a row,
Tech is a good place to go,
See all the things they make.

Food is great,
There is lots of fun,
Lots of games,
You can talk to your friends.

Classrooms always smell,
Some lessons are great,
PE is the most fun,
Play games all day long,
Some teachers are boring.

Chloe Bailey (13)
The Thomas Aveling School

The Kestrel

The kestrel hovers all through the day,
It has no bother catching its prey,
The kestrel devours its prey,
It goes up beyond the clouds,
So nothing can see it stalking its prey,
The kestrel swoops down,
To chase after a small bird,
The kestrel takes it back to the nest,
It takes a bite,
And the chick eats the rest.

Simon Hird (13)
The Thomas Aveling School

Death In The Air

Germans dropping bombs upon the British allies,
The shock of lost limbs,
Signs of horror in people's eyes,
Noises of explosions from nearby bombs,
People screaming from toxic gas,
And the stench of the dead in the trenches,
A sad place to be in.

Casey Perry (14)
The Thomas Aveling School

Family

Family,
Argumentative, competitive,
Angry, happy, loving, caring, sad,
Dysfunctional.

Ayulie Dabor (11)
The Thomas Aveling School

Me

My mum says I'm a cloud,
Dark and filled with rain,
My dad says I'm his thunder,
Clapping again and again.

My brothers say I'm dopey,
So stupid, can't think or act,
My sister says I'm mad,
Stating obvious facts.

I say I'm none of these,
I say I'm the sky,
I can flip from blue to grey.

Hayley Parkin (13)
The Thomas Aveling School